The New York Times

COFFEE, TEA OR CROSSWORDS
75 Light and Easy Puzzles

Edited by Will Shortz

ST. MARTIN'S GRIFFIN ⚏ NEW YORK

ISBN-13: 978-0-312-37828-8
ISBN-10: 0-312-37828-9

First Edition: February 2008

10 9 8 7 6 5 4 3 2 1

The New York Times

COFFEE, TEA OR CROSSWORDS

ACROSS

1 Derby drink
6 Futile
10 Word with critical or Catholic
14 Tylenol competitor
15 Red resident of Sesame Street
16 Troubles
17 "Olympia" artist
18 Mies van der ___
19 Delete
20 Eddie Murphy/Nick Nolte double feature?
23 Indian honorific
24 Sales talk
25 "Come on in!"
29 Successor to Marshall on the Supreme Court
33 Part of a tuba's sound
34 Cheering loudly
37 [Oh . . . my . . . Lord!]
38 George Clooney/Brad Pitt double feature?
42 Bankruptcy cause
43 The Creator, in the Koran
44 Contents of some pits
45 Poem part
48 Words below the Lincoln Memorial
50 Actor Davis
53 Archipelago part
54 Jessica Alba/Chris Evans double feature?
60 Race created by H. G. Wells
61 "Some busy and insinuating rogue," in Shakespeare

62 Long-billed game bird
64 Overflow (with)
65 Dog team's burden
66 Garden bulbs
67 Wheel turner
68 Banks on a runway
69 And those that follow: Lat.

DOWN

1 Stuff
2 ___ Bator
3 Director Riefenstahl
4 Still
5 Leader of the Lost Boys
6 Exceedingly
7 At ___ for words
8 Comment from a person who digs

9 Warning sign
10 Bar exam subject?
11 Baseball family name
12 Score connector, in music
13 Retired fliers
21 Layers
22 [snicker]
25 They can help you carry a tune
26 "Be silent," musically
27 Biblical queendom
28 ___ care in the world
30 Glossy alternative
31 Dam location
32 Wear
35 Hole puncher

36 Move, informally
39 Never
40 "Eraserhead" star Jack
41 A train may go down it
46 When doubled, a Gabor
47 Basketball statistic
49 Young swan
51 G8 member
52 "The ___ Sanction"
54 Greek salad ingredient
55 "Family Ties" son
56 Carol
57 Conclusion
58 Hastens
59 Hwy. with tolls
63 Title for a person with a J.D.

by David Quarfoot and Mike Nothnagel

2

ACROSS

1 Musical marks
5 Potentially offensive
9 Doll for boys
14 Shaping tool
15 "Quo Vadis" role
16 "___ Mio"
17 Manor man
18 Some folk acts
19 Some BlackBerry reading
20 Captain Renault player in "Casablanca"
23 Those against
24 Software pkg. item
25 Actor Epps
27 ___ corpus
30 Different
33 ___ Amin in "The Last King of Scotland"
34 Slangy assents
37 Nancy who married Ronald Reagan
38 Reuners: Abbr.
40 When clocks are changed back from D.S.T. in the fall
42 Fixes the time on, as a clock
43 ___ none
45 Like some checking accounts
47 "Citizen X" actor
48 "It's possible"
50 Like some stares
52 Dept. of Labor div.
53 From the top
55 Film lover's channel
57 Oscar nominee for "Pinky," 1949
62 Tuscany city
64 Zone
65 Island do
66 Studio sign
67 Decree
68 Jay Gould railroad
69 Slapped in court?
70 Revival setting
71 Partner of cones

DOWN

1 1 on the Mohs scale
2 One on a pedestal
3 Pound of verse
4 Break down and then draw in
5 Like Cousteau's work
6 Prefix with transmitter
7 Tourney for all
8 "___ fan tutte"
9 Loses it
10 Philosophy "Enter Talking" autobiographer, 1986
11 "Enter Talking" autobiographer, 1986
12 Hodgepodge
13 They're caught in pots
21 Do-or-die time
22 NCO part
26 [sigh]
27 U. S. Grant's given first name
28 ___ Rogers St. Johns
29 Singer with the 1984 hit "Caribbean Queen"
30 B-52 org.
31 Symbols of highness
32 Op-Ed piece
35 Au's is 79
36 Theme of this puzzle
39 Shows disconsolateness
41 Electrical power unit
44 Listened to again
46 He directed Marlon
49 Went nowhere
51 One in a rack
53 Mountain home
54 Reap
55 Starting on
56 Certain iPod
58 Sword handle
59 Mark's replacement
60 Bookie's worry
61 Hauls to court
63 Never, in Nuremberg

by Bette Sue Cohen

ACROSS

1 Lhasa ___ (dog)
5 High Hollywood honor
10 Ice hockey venue
14 "All ___ is divided into three parts"
15 Distress signal
16 First garden
17 German auto
18 *Park ranger's worry
20 Czech or Croat
21 Speak from a soapbox
22 Lab eggs
23 *Conifer exudation
26 Hopped to it
28 Pals
29 Come in last
31 ___ Doria (ill-fated ship)
34 Vagrant
38 Gossip queen Barrett
39 Like the starts of the answers to the six starred clues
41 Supply-and-demand subj.
42 Lively horses
44 Sudden
46 Mama ___ of the Mamas and the Papas
47 Command for Rover
48 Former Iranian leaders
51 *Metaphor for dense fog
55 Kernel holder
56 Sum
60 Adjust the pitch of
61 *Large seed of the alligator pear
64 Abbr. before the name of a memo recipient
65 ___ Strauss & Co.
66 1970s music fad
67 53, in old Rome
68 Not guilty, e.g.
69 Shuteye
70 Nifty

DOWN

1 Visibly horrified
2 Sainted eighth-century pope
3 Khartoum's land
4 *Peace offering
5 Popular insect repellent
6 Sailing vessels
7 Caleb who wrote "The Alienist"
8 Length × width, for a rectangle
9 Breather
10 Ump
11 Moron
12 Chutzpah
13 Work, as dough
19 Josh
24 Seek damages from
25 Proverbs
27 *Crunchy item at a salad bar
29 Gen. Meade's foe at Gettysburg
30 Rococo
31 Dadaist Jean
32 Neither's partner
33 Crime scene evidence
34 ___ Moines
35 Post-op location
36 Badge wearer
37 Explosive inits.
40 B. & O. and Reading: Abbr.
43 Words before spell, shadow or wide net
45 Sheep's cry
47 Put together, as film
48 Where hair roots grow
49 Shack
50 Superior to
52 Certain belly button
53 Loosen, as a knot
54 Enclose, as farm animals
57 Ten to one, e.g.
58 Hard work
59 Church recess
62 Spy org.
63 Blouse or shirt

by J. K. Hummel

4

ACROSS
1 Say "thay," e.g.
5 "Say good night, ___"
11 Land in la mer
14 Western edge of the Pacific Rim
15 A lot of summer TV
16 Buck's mate
17 Beatles girl "filling in a ticket in her little white book"
18 Rooster alternative?
20 Fantastic comics hero!
22 From ___ Z
23 Tennis do-over
24 Elevate
26 Marisa of "My Cousin Vinny"
28 Addict
31 Afternoon event
32 Items worn with shorts
35 Crafts' partner
36 Excellent novel title character!
38 Once-in-a-blue-moon
40 Smokey's tag
41 Blood-typing letters
42 Monopoly card
43 2006 Brad Pitt film that was a Best Picture nominee
47 Interest piquer
49 Horizontally: Abbr.
51 Like Chopin's "Tristesse" étude
52 Stupendous mentalist!
57 French vacation spot
58 Smokes
59 Crew need
60 "Later"
61 "This one's ___"

62 Parliament V.I.P.s
63 Golf course features
64 Spanish aunts

DOWN
1 Rodeo need
2 Likes
3 "Cheers," for one
4 Carson's predecessor
5 Steepness
6 Sparked anew
7 Elegant horse
8 See 12-Down
9 "By the power vested ___ . . ."
10 Dutch artist noted for optical illusions
11 Second Commandment prohibition
12 Small 8-Down of hair
13 Cry upon seeing a property tax bill, maybe
19 Unilever soap brand
21 Beethoven wrote for her
25 Profs' helpers
27 To be, in Brest
28 Goaded
29 Stick with a knife
30 Villa d'___
33 Abhor
34 Spillane's "___ Jury"
35 Magician's start
36 Show dog workers
37 Buffalo N.H.L.er
38 Mos Def's music
39 Patriarch of Judaism

42 Asleep for a while
44 Kind of wax
45 Riddle
46 Monocles, basically
48 Disfigure
49 Ohio city where Alcoholics Anonymous was founded
50 Animal stomachs
53 Actor Novello
54 Nick at ___
55 Trait carrier
56 Sean Connery, e.g.
57 Vertex

by Kevan Choset

ACROSS

1 Disney pup
6 Peaty places
10 Money in Pretoria
14 Neighbors of radii
15 Caen's river
16 Suffix with buck
17 Pre-wedding rituals
20 Speaks ill of
21 Hard-to-find object, perhaps
22 Vintage
24 Took off on
25 Parents' retirement place?
30 Actors Hale Sr. and Jr.
32 Puts on
33 Refrain syllable
34 Totally smitten
35 Musical John
36 Timid creature
37 Bush or Kerry, collegiately
38 Do a double-take
39 "A Girl Reading" painter
40 Classic Omar Sharif role
43 Village Voice award
44 Punny Bennett
45 "Let's go!"
48 Paddock sounds
52 Apt title for this puzzle
56 Hummus holder
57 Soft seat
58 Ostrich cousins
59 Alone, in a way
60 Asian nation suffix
61 It may be set in Paris

DOWN

1 Two-handed lunch orders
2 Silent sort
3 Utter conclusion?
4 School of Buddhism
5 Lady of rank
6 "No fair!"
7 Boston rink legend
8 Econ. yardstick
9 "Mystic River" co-star, 2003
10 Not for tender eyes
11 Like the Negev
12 Seasonal song
13 Two caplets, maybe
18 Aspiring J.D.'s exam
19 Orchestra section
23 Coat anew
24 Lacking life
25 Tricks
26 Toothed bar
27 Alamogordo's county
28 Snack with a creme center
29 Place to trade
30 Getting on in life
31 Composer Édouard
35 Quality of a ghost town
36 Ace versus ace
38 Bomb defuser, maybe
39 Education, law, etc.
41 Morgue ID
42 Peddle
45 Limits
46 Forget, maybe
47 ___ Hari
49 Writer from Zanesville
50 Make sound
51 Zaire's Mobutu ___ Seko
53 Go to seed
54 "Son ___ gun!"
55 Booster

by Bruce Adams

ACROSS

1 Gadabout
6 Dads' counterpart
10 Disconcert
14 January, in Juárez
15 Jai ___
16 Desertlike
17 Like folks cared for by former congressman Bob?
19 Telephone sound
20 Whichever
21 Book after Joel
22 Infuriate
24 Use a swizzle stick
25 Street urchin
26 Pollux's twin
29 Man of steel?
33 Wedding site
34 Quick job in a barbershop
35 Short-term worker
36 Max of "The Beverly Hillbillies"
37 "___ enough!"
38 Part of a judge's workload
39 Gen. Bradley
40 Sports "zebras"
41 Little Pigs' count
42 Boy genius of juvenile fiction
44 Holders of pirate treasures
45 Sword handle
46 Not single-sex, as a school
47 Naval affirmative
50 Complete flop
51 "Steady as ___ goes"
54 Angel's instrument
55 Like funds gathered by singer Vikki?
58 Writer Wiesel
59 Math class, in brief
60 Trap
61 Patch up

62 When Romeo meets Juliet
63 Dwarfs' count

DOWN

1 McEntire of country and western
2 ___ even keel
3 Extremely
4 Do something boneheaded
5 The spit in a spit roast, e.g.
6 Country estate
7 Bygone G.M. make
8 Screen siren West
9 Pistols and such
10 Like a ball retrieved by actor Jamie?
11 Diva's delivery

12 Get but good
13 Upper hand
18 Kuwaiti leader
23 "Delta of Venus" writer Anaïs
24 Like clay molded by drummer Ringo?
25 Does a garçon's job
26 Explorer Sebastian
27 Texas battle site of 1836
28 Geyser's emission
29 Knitting or beadwork
30 First, second, third and reverse
31 "No more, thanks"
32 Sporting blades
34 Larceny
37 Racetrack bet

41 Springsteen, to fans
43 Modus operandi
44 Freebie
46 Welsh dog
47 "Uh . . . excuse me"
48 Ivy League school
49 Land of leprechauns
50 Londoner or Liverpudlian, e.g.
51 Eastern European
52 "Kilroy was ___"
53 Genesis garden
56 Path of a javelin
57 White Monopoly bill

by Randall J. Hartman

ACROSS

1 Language of Libya
7 Food flavor enhancer, for short
10 Amo, ___, amat . . .
14 Number of feet between baseball bases
15 Mock, in a way
16 Streamlet
17 *Chicken
19 Sedgwick of Warhol films
20 Latin "behold"
21 Just about forever
22 Scout's quest
23 *Very good child
27 Tiny hill dweller
28 Tiebreakers, briefly
29 Not so sure
31 Guard
35 It lets things go
38 You might R.S.V.P. online to this
39 Contributed to
40 Celtic priest
41 Snugglers
43 Reddish-brown
44 "Die Lorelei" poet
45 Vietnam Memorial designer
46 World Series mo.
48 *Venus
54 Drastic sentence, with "the"
56 Judge pro ___
57 Cart puller
58 Parking meter filler
59 *Purple sandwich filler
62 Addresses starting http://
63 Peach center
64 ___ Mae (college money provider)
65 Pause
66 Part of a milit. address
67 Ethan and Woody

DOWN

1 Photographer Adams
2 Designer Nina
3 Put on ___ (fake it)
4 Special Forces headwear
5 Suffix with meteor
6 Charisse of "Singin' in the Rain"
7 City nicknamed "Heart of Georgia"
8 Sparkly
9 Play a good joke on
10 Region
11 *Short shadow caster
12 Make parallel
13 Street slickener
18 First half of a Senate vote
22 Obviously injured
24 More isolated
25 Airport info: Abbr.
26 Wriggler
30 Like an ivory-billed woodpecker
31 Hibernation spot
32 Noted apple eater
33 Has the rear end move side to side . . . or a hint to the five asterisked clues
34 Suffix with kitchen
35 ___ judicata
36 Germanic one
37 Cereal box fig.
39 Frequent flier's reward
42 Ltr. holder
43 Sloth, e.g.
45 Unfirm
46 Take place
47 Ironing, for one
49 "Keen!"
50 Stink
51 Veil material
52 Tuckered out
53 Spanish kings
55 Mass. ___ of Tech.
59 No. on a transcript
60 That one, in Tijuana
61 Major Asian carrier, for short

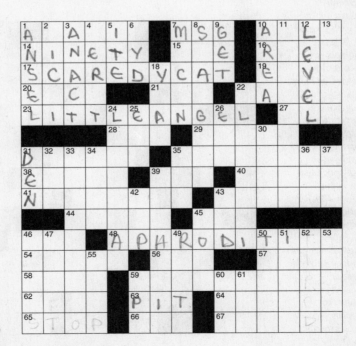

by Jennifer Nutt

ACROSS

1 Playground retort
6 Pre-bedtime ritual
10 Flower people?: Abbr.
13 Passes over
14 Made an overthrow, say
16 Milne baby
17 Rectory
19 Coastal bird
20 Super server
21 Multivolume refs.
22 Neckline?
24 Minor-league club, in baseball
26 Jumper alternative
28 Locked up
32 Make secure
33 Christopher of "Back to the Future"
34 Kinski title role
36 Look after
39 Delicacy that may be pickled
40 Worthless pile
43 Fish spawn
44 Speaker in the Hall of Fame
46 "___ were . . ."
47 Easy pace
49 Keep one's distance from
51 Glare blocker
53 Erudite sort
56 Foot specialist?
57 ___ water
58 Part of A.A.R.P.: Abbr.
60 Autocrat of old
64 ___ fault
65 Feast of Trumpets
68 Balance provider, for short
69 ___-Detoo
70 Sounds to shop by
71 Hi-___ monitor
72 Harsh cry
73 Tickle

DOWN

1 L-___ (treatment for parkinsonism)
2 Apple variety
3 Desperate
4 Wok preparation
5 Bygone covert org.
6 Whales, elephants, etc.
7 Dominican-American major-league slugger, to fans
8 Tie up tightly
9 Cock and bull
10 Sprigs from the garden
11 Sculpted form
12 "___ disturb!" (and a hint for 17-, 40- and 65-Across and 10- and 30-Down)
15 American rival
18 ___ de combat
23 Tel. message taker, maybe
25 1953 Loren title role
27 Mrs. Einstein
28 "Why should ___ you?"
29 D-back, for one
30 Deli selections
31 Classic sodas
35 Go into business
37 Court plea, for short
38 They're game
41 Mideast capital
42 Cobble, for example
45 "Amscray!"
48 "The Night of the Hunter" star, 1955
50 To-the-max prefix
52 Hendryx of the group Labelle
53 "Norwegian Wood" instrument
54 Franklin's on it
55 Dreadlocked one
59 Keep an appointment
61 Bird in "The Lion King"
62 Literary olios
63 Croupier's tool
66 Suffix with direct
67 Little, to a lass

by Jim Page

ACROSS

1 Like some 1930s design, informally
5 Mafia biggie
9 Light from a lightning bug, e.g.
13 ___ Gay (W.W. II plane)
15 Worm's place on a fishing line
16 Make over
17 3"×5" aids for speakers
19 Out of control
20 Take to court
21 Formerly, old-style
22 Sky-blue
23 Corporate office staffers
27 WNW's opposite
28 Elevator company
29 Shut loudly
32 Des Moines native
34 ET's craft
37 Identify exactly . . . or a hint to this puzzle's theme
41 Lumberjacking tool
42 Edgar ___ Poe
43 It might be slapped after a good joke
44 Writer ___ Stanley Gardner
45 New Year's ___
47 Fonzie's girl on "Happy Days"
54 Surrenders
55 Leo's symbol
56 Ph.D., e.g.: Abbr.
57 End-___ (ultimate buyer)
58 Head of a cabal
61 Doe's mate
62 Tehran's land
63 Add liquor to, as punch
64 Roly-___
65 Mishmash
66 "___ of the D'Urbervilles"

DOWN

1 Basic religious belief
2 Boredom
3 In secret language
4 Encouragement for a matador
5 Deep gap
6 Main artery
7 Pea holder
8 10-4's
9 Barely injures in passing
10 Cousin of a monkey
11 Stinks
12 Regained consciousness
14 Figure skating jumps
18 Indian of the northern Plains
22 Getting on in years
24 Record sent to a record producer
25 Hopeless, as a situation
26 ___ all-time high
29 Site of mineral waters
30 Illumination unit
31 Dined
32 Bit of land in the sea
33 Birds ___ feather
34 Vase
35 Enemy
36 Last number in a countdown
38 Drug agents: Var.
39 ___ May of "The Beverly Hillbillies"
40 Scraped (out)
44 Cabinet department since 1977
45 E.P.A. subj.
46 Barn toppers
47 Sauce in un ristorante
48 Perfect
49 Arm bones
50 Omens
51 Murphy who's heard in "Shrek"
52 Stinks
53 Meanies
54 Edge
58 Edge
59 Wrath
60 Fitting

by David Pringle

ACROSS

1 Rude sorts
6 Play a kazoo
9 Fix, as a photocopier
14 Naval convoy menace
15 Prefix with metric
16 Supercool
17 Pitcher of baseball's Gas House Gang
19 Speedpass-accepting gas company
20 Old codger
21 Exactly
23 Man of Steel's symbol
24 Says
27 Pass along, as an e-mail: Abbr.
30 Golf's 1984 U.S. Open winner
33 Dines
36 Top-shelf
37 Signs to heed
38 Sleep phase, for short
40 Cottage cheese, essentially
41 Ibuprofen target
42 Lunchtimes, typically
44 Patriarch on an MTV reality show
48 Born, on the society page
49 Skier's lodging
50 Draft org.
53 Like an eagle's vision
54 "Same goes for me"
57 With "cum" and 32-Down, a diploma phrase
60 The Fresh Prince's partner DJ
63 How the confident solve

64 Eggs, in labs
65 Really bother
66 Really bothers, with "at"
67 Equinox mo.
68 Girlie man

DOWN

1 Move a bit
2 Theater awards since 1956
3 Moves like molasses
4 Bronx cheer
5 Eyelid woe
6 Hotfoot it
7 ___ Today
8 Exotic dancer Lola
9 Fidgety feeling
10 Barber's call
11 The Jaguars, on scoreboards

12 ___ Z (the gamut)
13 Start of the work wk., for many
18 Syrian/Lebanese religious group
22 ___ y plata
25 Russian autocrat: Var.
26 Popular reliever of aches
27 Fauna's partner
28 "Peter Pan" heroine
29 Get decked out
30 Keister
31 Vocal stumbles
32 See 57-Across
33 Motorcyclist's invitation
34 Knock the socks off
35 Take forcibly
39 Pouty look

40 Anderson Cooper's channel
43 Baseball's David, nicknamed "Big Papi"
45 Vast amounts
46 That ship
47 Dixieland instruments
50 "Keep it in" notations
51 Love seats, e.g.
52 Kindhearted sort
53 Had down pat
55 Tattooist's supply
56 Town near Santa Barbara
57 Russian fighter
58 Cape ___, Mass.
59 4.0 is a great one
61 Forum greeting
62 Microwave

by Brendan Emmett Quigley

ACROSS

1 King who united England
7 Game period: Abbr.
10 Hinged closer
14 Friend
15 Laramie's state: Abbr.
16 They lean to the right: Abbr.
17 Teleologist's concern
20 Word on a Mexican stop sign
21 Bugged
22 French flower
23 1/100 of a euro
24 Vainglory
25 On the side of
26 Part of the verb "to be," to Popeye
28 Overlook
32 "September 1, 1939" poet
35 Old Asian ruler
37 Jaffa's land: Abbr.
38 Figuring something out
42 A hallucinogen
43 Hanging ___ a thread
44 August 15, 1945
45 Nosedive
47 Indent setter
48 Carrier with the in-flight magazine Scanorama
49 Actress Gardner
51 Cries during a paso doble
53 "It's not TV. It's ___"
56 Make worse
60 Clunker of a car
61 Part of a city code
63 Bring to naught
64 Give the coup de grâce
65 Lamebrain, in slang
66 ___ extra cost

67 Some ESPN highlights, for short
68 Oliver Twist and others

DOWN

1 Like two dimes and four nickels
2 Without much intelligence
3 Actress Naomi of "Mulholland Dr."
4 Sony co-founder Morita
5 Post-retirement activity?
6 Bureau part
7 Places to find the letters circled in the grid
8 Use 7-Down
9 Worker who makes rounds
10 Zoo heavyweights, informally
11 On
12 MS. enclosure
13 Argued (for)
18 10th anniversary gift
19 Scandal sheet
23 Neighbor of Gabon
25 Quagmire
27 Sounds leading up to a sneeze
29 Pirate captain of legend
30 La Española, e.g.
31 Hunted animals
32 "___ Lang Syne"
33 U.S. ally in W.W. II
34 One-named singer with the 2001 hit "Thank You"
36 Exploding stars

39 Meeting expectations
40 Cagers' grp.
41 Breakfast drinks, for short
46 "Scent of a Woman" Oscar winner
48 Going out with
50 Title for one on the way to sainthood: Abbr.
52 British "Inc."
53 Artist Matisse
54 Strips for breakfast
55 Some opinion pieces
56 Old Testament book
57 Eliminate
58 Have ___ with
59 It both precedes and follows James
60 Soccer star Mia
62 Actress Long

by John Farmer

ACROSS

1 King Kong's kin
5 Dry out
10 Aspen gear
14 N.Y.C. cultural center
15 Big name in can-making
16 Tight curl
17 Elastic holder
19 Opposed to
20 Depart's opposite
21 Lisa, to Bart
23 Actor Beatty
24 "Cheers" woman
25 Home of Notre Dame
28 Abbr. at the end of a company's name
29 1986 Indy 500 winner Bobby
31 Clear, as a chalkboard
32 S-shaped molding
34 Three Stooges laugh
35 Dreaded
36 Entrance, as through oratory
39 Macaroni and manicotti
42 Landon who ran for president in 1936
43 1978 hit with the lyric "You can get yourself clean, you can have a good meal"
47 Non-earthling
48 Win the first four games in a World Series, e.g.
50 Gear part
51 Ian Fleming creation
53 "Filthy" money
55 Stereo component
56 Deviation in a rocket's course
57 Actor Brando
58 Miniature plateau
60 1930s political group
63 Bustles
64 Filmmaker Coen
65 Neighborhood
66 Lost seaworthiness
67 Eccentric
68 Separators on badminton courts

DOWN

1 Medium for mostly news and talk these days
2 Raining cats and dogs
3 Hug
4 Polio vaccine developer
5 Whittle down
6 Priest's vestment
7 Color TV pioneer
8 Certain diplomat
9 "I've ___!" (cry of impatience)
10 Jamaican music
11 Greg of "You've Got Mail"
12 Strong, as emotions
13 Lost control of a car, say
18 At any time
22 Luster
25 Synagogue
26 Chicago suburb
27 Two-time Super Bowl M.V.P. Tom
30 Affirmative votes
33 ___ Lauder cosmetics
35 Flute in a march
37 Variety of violet
38 Ran in the wash
39 Nightclothes
40 Oakland's county
41 Bart or Lisa
44 Doug of "The Virginian"
45 Royal headgear
46 Lists for meetings
48 Part of Johannesburg
49 Schedule
52 Item on which to put lox
54 City-related
57 Quite a few
59 Query
61 Letter between pi and sigma
62 Rand McNally product

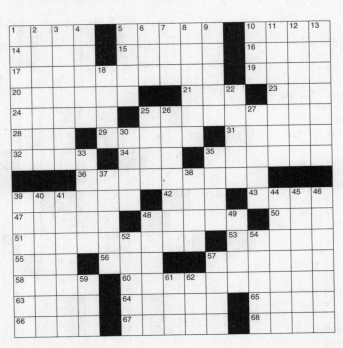

by Allan E. Parrish

ACROSS

1 Drink garnishes
6 Seizes
11 "How about that?!"
14 Broadcast workers' org.
15 Lash of bygone westerns
16 Former
17 Antic brother
19 Fish story
20 Stitched
21 Raw resource
22 Pack, to a pack animal
24 Sticking one's nose in
27 Canine line
28 Swan's mate, in myth
29 Order in the court
33 Brigitte's friends
36 Seattle-to-Phoenix dir.
37 Sci-fi invaders
38 Title of this puzzle
43 What Alabama cheerleaders say to "gimme" four times
44 Alley ___
45 "Is there no ___ this?"
46 Speaks when one should stay out
49 Tidy up topside
51 Inspiring sound
52 Like many Chas Addams characters
56 Dinner table item on a string
59 '07, '08 and '09
60 Onetime E.P.A. target
62 Chinese dynasty
63 Back
66 Non-Rx
67 Absurd
68 Coffee for bedtime
69 Play for a fool
70 Wild
71 Clifford who co-wrote "Sweet Smell of Success"

DOWN

1 Takes a sharp turn
2 Violinist Zimbalist
3 Vermont ski town
4 Rolled along
5 Animal pouch
6 Praise from a choir
7 Nagano noodles
8 Heavenly altar
9 Bedroom community, briefly
10 Like some relations
11 Place to pick up valuable nuggets
12 Peace Nobelist Wiesel
13 Heaven on earth
18 Phone button
23 School basics, initially?
25 Arnaz of '50s TV
26 Big cut
30 Author Harper
31 Leave in, in proofreading
32 Petrol brand
33 Quatrain rhyme scheme
34 PC pop-up
35 Mesmerized
36 Big inits. at Indy
39 "___ certainly do not!"
40 1970s TV's "The ___ Show"
41 Down-to-earth
42 Without an agenda
47 Check
48 Zhivago portrayer
49 Equine color
50 Milquetoast
53 "Laughing" scavenger
54 Pizzeria order
55 Tore into
56 10 C-notes
57 Absorbs, as a loss
58 "The Match Game" host Rayburn
61 Makes calls
64 Alternative spelling: Abbr.
65 Tokyo, once

by Courtenay Crocker and Nancy Salomon

14

ACROSS

1 Rock's Green Day, for one
5 Worker during a walkout
9 First-stringers
14 Hebrides island
15 Manger visitors
16 Pulitzer Prize category
17 Closet pest
18 Concerning
19 Long-billed wader
20 Coin thrown for good luck?
23 Work started by London's Philological Soc.
24 Geeky guy
25 Grand Canyon beast
29 All lit up
31 Letterman letters
34 Kurds and Nepalis
36 My ___, Vietnam
37 Stones from the sky
38 Result of sitting on a court bench too long?
41 "The Morning Watch" author
42 River to the Rhine
43 Feed for livestock
44 Neurotic TV dog
45 Lusted after, visually
47 Palette choice
48 Scott Turow work set at Harvard
49 Sound of amazement
51 Bugged Bugs?
57 Edible shells
58 Neighbor of an Arkie
59 Projecting edge
61 Waters seen on Broadway
62 Creatures of habit?
63 Pinnacle
64 Shade of gray
65 Learned
66 Battery component

DOWN

1 The youngest Cratchit
2 It may be raised
3 Having as a hobby
4 Waikiki locale
5 Deal a mighty blow
6 Dudley Do-Right's home
7 Cultural beginning?
8 Like House elections
9 Stick
10 What a line on a chart may show
11 Be worthy of
12 Taiwan Strait city
13 Answer to the riddle of the Sphinx
21 Before Oedipus, who could answer the riddle of the Sphinx
22 Risks
25 Storybook elephant
26 Subject of Fowler's handbook
27 Up
28 Make copiously, with "in"
30 "Accident ahead" indicator
31 Alimentary ___
32 "You got it!"
33 Less straightforward
35 One putting on a show
37 Holy ring
39 Puffs out
40 Woman's shoulder wrap
45 Standing by
46 Plying with pills
48 Cousin of a mink
50 Much too big for one's britches?
51 "Haughty Juno's unrelenting ___": Dryden
52 Labor Dept. arm
53 Arctic bird
54 Well-executed
55 Mane site
56 The "Y" of Y.S.L.
57 Zing
60 Bus. phone line

by Richard Silvestri

ACROSS

1 Base on balls
5 Lowly chess piece
9 Afro-Brazilian dance
14 Nastase of tennis
15 Feel sore
16 "___ Gold" (1997 film)
17 See 18-Across
18 Grand ___ (annual French auto 17-Across)
19 "Carmen" composer
20 "The Breakfast Club" actor
23 Preceder of com or org
24 Desperately needing a map
25 Dangerous person
28 Donkey
29 Officer's honorific
30 '60s war site
31 More work than required
36 Lyricist Gershwin
37 "Um, excuse me"
38 "Foucault's Pendulum" author
39 The "A" in ABM
40 "My mama done ___ me"
41 It may come as a shock to a diver
45 Put to a purpose
46 Accomplished
47 French vacation time
48 Argentine grassland
50 Be wide-open
52 Salary
55 Domain ruled from Constantinople
58 Actor John of "The Addams Family"
60 ___ California
61 Pastel shade

62 Michaels of "S.N.L."
63 Brilliant display
64 Bath fixtures
65 Philadelphia N.H.L.er
66 Burden of proof
67 Radiator output

DOWN

1 Sent by telegraph
2 1836 battle site
3 Permissible
4 Part of a hull
5 Native American baby
6 Farm units
7 Early form of bridge
8 Cry at a motor vehicle bureau
9 Undermine

10 Green card holder
11 Floor between first and second
12 Spell-off
13 Winter hrs. in Bermuda
21 Ingrid's role in "Casablanca"
22 Ruler of Qatar
26 ___ blanche
27 Communication that may have an attachment
28 Sleeve filler
29 Chimney sweep's target
31 Devour hungrily
32 South African native
33 Rocket data
34 Nourish
35 TV watchdog: Abbr.

39 Good card to have "in the hole"
41 Lou Grant portrayer
42 Santa checks his twice, in song
43 Second airings
44 Topic of gossip
49 Thomas who wrote "Common Sense"
50 Corn or oat
51 Pear variety
52 Tickle, as one's interest
53 Dutch-speaking Caribbean island
54 It makes dough rise
56 Spanish river to the Mediterranean
57 Trail
58 TV extraterrestrial
59 Note between fa and la

by Janet Bender

ACROSS
1 French girlfriend
5 Karate strokes
10 Laugh uproariously
14 Suburban gathering place
15 Capital of Vietnam
16 Song for Dame Nellie Melba
17 One not taking just a few classes
20 Catholic prayer book
21 Avoid contact with
22 Lines of praise
23 401, in Roman times
25 Many a sword-and-sandals film
27 Magazine with the recurring heading "Onward and Upward With the Arts," with "The"
32 Comedian Fields
36 Eight: Sp.
37 Snakelike fish
38 Typo, e.g.
39 Large number
40 Polish receivers
43 El ___ (weather phenomenon)
44 Country/rock singer Steve
46 Noted Bronx locale
47 Wife of Geraint
48 Mill output
49 Kind of sale
51 Decorations on some rearview mirrors
53 Supped
54 Giant great Mel
57 "Gone With the Wind" setting

59 One of four in "America"
64 Starts of 17-, 27- and 49-Across
67 Bridge or foot feature
68 Emcee's delivery
69 It's a "terrible thing to waste"
70 Relative of a mandolin
71 Actor Davis of "Jungle Fever"
72 Lode stones

DOWN
1 Radio button
2 Lanai neighbor
3 Woes
4 Right angles
5 Offspring
6 Amateur radioer
7 Change for a five

8 More luxurious
9 Stomach strengthener
10 Bamboozled
11 Hydrox rival, once
12 Oboe, e.g.
13 Likely to miss the bus, say
18 Tex-Mex staple
19 Join forces
24 Retail furniture chain
26 Where ends meet
27 Beaks
28 Brilliance of performance
29 Info on an invitation
30 Cried out in pain
31 Doolittle of fiction
33 Singer Lopez
34 Column style
35 Wear away

41 Kinks hit with a spelled-out title
42 Quiet tap dancing
45 Type smaller than pica
49 Some long-legged birds
50 Townshend of the Who
52 Big name in calculators and digital watches
54 Translucent gem
55 No ___ Traffic
56 Diplomacy
58 Early p.m.'s
60 BB's, e.g.
61 Bet that's not rouge
62 District
63 &&&&
65 ___-wolf
66 Prefix with angle

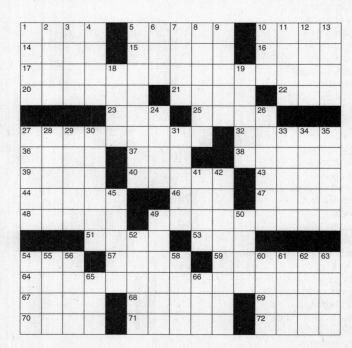

by Sarah Keller

17

ACROSS

1 Churn
5 Tale with a point
10 Pre-Communist leader
14 It's a killer
15 Tubular instruments
16 Doing
17 Winston Churchill's description of a fanatic, part 1
19 Gymnastics apparatus, for short
20 Layout
21 Opposite of Mar. on a calendar
23 American Depression, e.g.
24 Part of A/C
25 Secured, as a fish on a line
27 Description, part 2
31 Suffer
32 Not the brainiest sort
33 December celebrations
36 Chooses
39 Dreadful
41 Rock's ___ Van Halen
42 Lug
43 "Lead ___ King Eternal" (hymn)
44 Description, part 3
49 How often federal elections are held
51 Science fiction author Stanislaw
52 "Well, ___ be!"
53 Free (of)
54 Formally speaks
58 Résumé addenda
60 Description's end
63 Rangy
64 Like a despot, typically
65 Western Indian
66 Pushing the envelope
67 Collars worn outside the lapels
68 Payment in Monopoly

DOWN

1 Part of the mouth
2 "Yes ___?"
3 Froster
4 Tin star wearer
5 Barber chair feature
6 "Dancing With the Stars" airer
7 It has some feathers around the neck
8 Contacts, e.g.
9 Revere
10 Margarine container
11 Leadfoot
12 Pong creator
13 Not italic
18 Alexander who said "I'm in control here"
22 "Elder" of ancient history
25 Tear (up)
26 Orbiting chimp of 1961
27 Legal assignment
28 Double-timed
29 From dawn till dusk
30 Owns
34 "Metropolis" director Fritz
35 Gin fruit
37 "Bild" article
38 Moth deterrent
39 Bldg. unit
40 Obscures
42 Indiscriminate amount
45 Squirm
46 Commonplace
47 Spearmint, e.g.
48 Key with three sharps
49 Oath taker's aid
50 Classic epic
55 Head, in an école
56 College course, briefly
57 Mark indicating "O.K. as is"
59 Heavens
61 Abbr. on W.W. II maps
62 Bayh or Biden: Abbr.

by Patrick Merrell

18

ACROSS
1 Some Apple computers
6 Fall behind
9 Milan's La ___
14 End of an Aesop fable
15 Eggs
16 Secret languages
17 *Mock rock band in a 1984 film
19 From the country
20 Hides the gray
21 Old-fashioned "Scram!"
22 "Dear" dispenser of advice
25 *Revealer of vowels, on TV
28 Hardly trim
30 Enclosure for grain or coal
31 "Cut it out!"
32 Hearing-related
33 Hawaiian veranda
35 *Part of a Valentine's Day bouquet
37 *Seasoned seaman
42 The mating game?
44 Rarin' to go
45 Citrus coolers
49 Parts of lbs.
50 Tie the knot
51 *Local place for making deposits or getting loans
54 ___ empty stomach
55 Garb
56 Long, long time
58 Around, as a year
59 Be logical . . . or what the last words of the answers to the five starred clues can do?

64 Parts of eyes
65 Nothing's opposite
66 Rub out
67 Oozes
68 "Affirmative"
69 Pub projectiles

DOWN
1 Quick online notes, for short
2 Clean the floor
3 ___ Onassis, Jackie Kennedy's #2
4 Butterfinger or 3 Musketeers
5 Smite
6 "___ luck!"
7 Gardner of "The Night of the Iguana"
8 Space between the teeth, e.g.

9 Fastener that turns
10 Robitussin suppresses them
11 Skillful
12 Crude shelter
13 Dozing
18 Impose, as a tax
21 Yawn-inspiring
22 From quite a distance
23 Azure
24 Poet
26 Org. with a 24-second shot clock
27 Bogotá boys
29 Voting coalition
33 Talk show host Gibbons
34 Notion
36 Ocean's edge
38 Tokyo "ta-ta!"

39 Not fer
40 Mother of Helen, in myth
41 1982 sci-fi film
43 Tax ID
45 You can always count on this
46 Latin case
47 Course before dessert
48 Headwear on the slopes
50 Place for a lawn mower
52 Military bigwigs
53 Phones
57 Was in debt
59 Stable diet?
60 Cheer for a matador
61 Road surface
62 Ballpark fig.
63 High-___ monitor

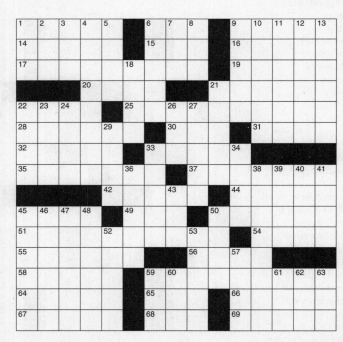

by Paula Gamache

ACROSS

1 Baseball's Rose
5 Struck, old-style
9 Violin master Zimbalist
14 Nike competitor
15 ___ Hari (infamous spy)
16 Native New Zealander
17 Super-easy decision
19 Carpet cleaner target
20 Tightwads
22 Dino whose body was more than 30 feet long
23 Vote in a legislative body
24 Official, informally
25 In ___ (as found)
27 Noted Charlton Heston role
29 Aunts' relatives
33 Reverent
36 Put too much pressure on
38 Gremlins and Pacers
39 Eyelid woes
40 "Dumb ___" (old comic strip)
41 Get the sniffles
43 Place with a "do or dye" situation?
44 Having an uninterrupted series of steps
45 Like 5:00 or 6:00 a.m., say
47 P.T.A. concern: Abbr.
49 Gray general
50 Full-bodied quaff
53 Electrical letters
56 Really, really dumb
59 Kitchen wrap
61 Recycled metal
62 Score with two balls
63 Body art, slangily
64 Singer Horne
65 "That's a lie!"
66 Accessory for Miss America
67 Places to tone bodies

DOWN

1 Garden bloom
2 Conjure up
3 Part of the lower body skeleton
4 Make, as a salary
5 Beams
6 Unabomber's writing, e.g.
7 Major Calif.-to-Fla. route
8 Fruity desserts
9 Grp. called after an accident
10 Big Easy bash
11 Surf sound
12 Buffalo's body of water
13 Flirt
18 Hairdos for Jimi Hendrix and others
21 Trig ratios
26 "My country, ___ of thee"
27 G.T.O.s, e.g.
28 Flair
30 Hip
31 Money since 2002
32 "South Park" boy who's always crying "Oh my God, they killed Kenny!"
33 Big donors to office seekers
34 G3 or G4 computer
35 Eight: Prefix
37 Enterprise warnings
39 Clean with elbow grease
42 Made a fool of
43 Get some shuteye
46 Same old stuff
48 Prices
50 One selling TV time, e.g.
51 Hotelier Helmsley
52 Author Ferber and others
53 Members' body: Abbr.
54 Mob boss
55 "Dagnabbit!"
57 Final Four org.
58 Suffers bodily woes
60 Hero of "The Matrix"

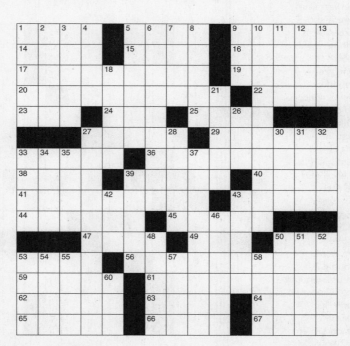

by John Halverson

ACROSS

1 Birthplace of Galileo
5 Up
10 Not much
14 Bad time for Caesar
15 Word with press or Marine
16 Broccoli ___ (leafy vegetable)
17 Thrill
19 Critical hosp. areas
20 Close communication?
21 Emmy winner for "Chicago Hope"
22 Couple
23 Part of a chemistry group
25 Conservatory graduate
28 Heartless one?
31 Companion of 28-Across
32 It merged with Mobil
36 Plane prefix
37 Seaport of New Guinea
38 Part of a coach's chalk-talk diagram
39 Start of a countdown
40 Baseball's Ed and Mel
42 ". . . like a ___ chocolates"
44 Tennis great Lacoste
45 Bernstein's "Trouble in ___"
47 Eye passionately
49 Jong who wrote "Fanny"
51 Boohoo
52 Roman septet
54 Flo Ziegfeld's specialty
59 Athens's setting
60 "Piece of cake!" (and a hint to the starts of 17-Across and 11- and 27-Down)
61 Musical Mitchell
62 One of Homer's in-laws
63 Maglie and Mineo
64 Diner sign
65 On pins and needles
66 Give out

DOWN

1 Willis's "Twelve Monkeys" co-star
2 Romeo's last words
3 Group of prayers
4 Didn't leave waiting at the door
5 Film overlay
6 Imbibed
7 One who watches the telly
8 Breathing problem
9 "Ba-a-a-ad!"
10 Huffington who wrote "Fanatics & Fools"
11 Part of a dash
12 Go up against
13 Half a classic sitcom couple
18 Places
21 Year before Trajan was born
24 Fuji, e.g.: Abbr.
25 Apportion
26 Rope with a slipknot
27 Do what is expected
29 Sporting site
30 Three trios
33 Kiss and hugs, in a love letter
34 Adults-only
35 Big name in kitchen gadgets
41 Certain cut
42 Certain razor
43 June 14
44 Medical setback
46 "___ a pity"
48 Mas with baas
50 Blanched
51 Soothers
52 Breakfast spot, briefly
53 Breakfast spot, briefly
55 Feature of the earth
56 Quahog, e.g.
57 Anklebones
58 Part of DOS: Abbr.
60 Gen. Lee's cause

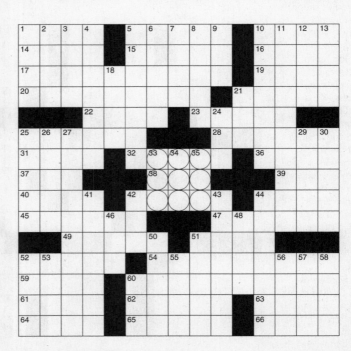

by Patrick Blindauer

ACROSS

1 Late bridge columnist Truscott
5 Cry made with a flourish
9 ___ Park, Colo.
14 Of sound mind
15 Cheers for toreros
16 Seismic occurrence
17 Supreme Court justice known for a literalist interpretation of the Bill of Rights
19 Earthy pigment
20 Flub
21 Employee cards with photos, e.g.
22 Squad with red, white and blue uniforms
24 Deny
26 Three-card ___
27 Public square
29 Infer (from)
33 Analyze, as ore
36 Perry Mason's creator ___ Stanley Gardner
38 Eurasian duck
39 Cut, as a lawn
40 Los Angeles N.B.A.er
41 Yellowfin, e.g.
42 Jai ___
43 "Break ___!" ("Good luck!")
44 Violin bow application
45 Thrill-seeker's watercraft
47 Subject
49 Tom who played Forrest Gump
51 Former mayor who wrote "Mayor"
55 Emancipate
58 Show the effect of weight
59 Syllable repeated after "hot"
60 Napoleon on St. Helena, e.g.
61 Pie filling
64 Fracas
65 Winnie-the-___
66 Auto racer Yarborough
67 Religion of the Koran
68 Popular frozen dessert chain
69 Signs, as a contract

DOWN

1 Pale-faced
2 First lady after Hillary
3 Red-faced, maybe
4 Prefix with conservative
5 "What'd I say?!"
6 "___, poor Yorick! I knew him, Horatio"
7 Follower of Nov.
8 Provide an invitation for
9 Consider identical
10 Some theater productions
11 Perfume brand
12 Barely makes, with "out"
13 Antitoxins
18 Onion-flavored roll
23 Follower of rear or week
25 1966 Herb Alpert & the Tijuana Brass hit
26 What the last words of 17- and 61-Across and 10- and 25-Down are kinds of
28 Ardor
30 Don of morning radio
31 "___, vidi, vici"
32 Actor McGregor
33 Key related to F# minor: Abbr.
34 Only
35 Go for, as a fly
37 Toy block brand
40 Frankie who sang "Mule Train"
44 Chain of hills
46 Hoops great Abdul-Jabbar
48 A-O.K.
50 Well-groomed
52 Surfing spot
53 Writer on a slate
54 Loathes
55 Vehicle that can jackknife
56 Alimony receivers, e.g.
57 Cash register
58 Look-down-one's-nose type
62 Quadrennial games grp.
63 Sprint rival

by Allan E. Parrish

ACROSS

1 "Listen!"
5 Covered with water
10 Underwater growth
14 On deep water
15 Plan that stinks
17 Doe, in song
19 Art supporters?
20 Three-time U.S. Open champ
21 Pittsburgh product
22 Pickle juice
24 Tiny
27 Teeny-tiny distance
29 Greenish-blue
30 Computer program, for short
33 General Motors subsidiary
34 Light
36 Ray, in song
39 One of the Quad Cities, in Illinois
40 Stage assistant
41 Resort
42 "What's ___ for me?"
43 Money, slangily
45 Private eye, slangily
46 Nonsense
48 Charged particle
52 Spirit of a culture
54 Boxing combo
55 Me, in song
59 Modern computer feature
60 "Peter Pan" pirate
61 Queue
62 Muscat-eer?
63 Spanish direction

DOWN

1 Pluto's alias
2 "Have ___" (host's words)
3 Oscar-winning Witherspoon
4 N.B.A. first name that's Arabic for "noble" or "exalted"
5 Barks
6 Misery
7 Bill provider, for short
8 Red star?
9 Trojan captive
10 William the pirate
11 Alpine flower
12 Entertainer Pinky or Peggy
13 Average
16 Hawaiian goose
18 "___ Road," 1994 hit by the Gin Blossoms
22 Talk big
23 1987 sci-fi film set in near-future Detroit
25 Eagerly devour
26 Actress Verdugo
28 Rick's ___ Américain, "Casablanca" setting
29 Old cable inits.
30 Let in
31 Lying facedown
32 One dressed in blue
34 ___ fixe
35 1990 reunification site
37 Cockfight area
38 Bait
43 Drop one's weapon
44 Real
46 "Don't breathe a word of ___"
47 Golfer Mediate
49 Parts of a list
50 Little hooter
51 Lacking a charge
53 French noodle?
54 Prefix with potent
55 Gridiron org.
56 "The Greatest"
57 Meadow
58 Author Deighton

by Roger Wolff

ACROSS

1 Moisten, in a way
6 Q-tip, e.g.
10 In the sack
14 Really enjoyed
15 Sign of a saint
16 MS. accompanier
17 Junction points
18 Yemeni port
19 Part of a bird's gullet
20 Org. with a noted journal
21 Start of a quip from a hunter
24 Composer Rimsky-Korsakov
26 "___ hath an enemy called Ignorance": Ben Jonson
27 Quip, part 2
33 One putting out feelers?
34 Visa alternative, informally
35 "Little piggy"
36 Partner of trembling
39 Person with a code name, maybe
40 Fraction of a euro
41 Clumsy ox
42 Pump, e.g.
44 Federal property agcy.
46 Quip, part 3
52 Gal of song
53 Be fond of
54 End of the quip
59 Pa. nuclear plant site
60 Word repeated in a Doris Day song
61 Spring shape
62 Little laugh
64 Not of the cloth
65 Russian city on the Oka
66 Not pimply
67 Tram loads
68 Forms a union
69 Solving helpers

DOWN

1 Yogurt flavor
2 Like some energy
3 Neil who wrote "Stupid Cupid"
4 Calendar column: Abbr.
5 Delta follower
6 See 25-Down
7 Dry riverbed
8 Protected, in a way
9 Slave's state
10 Fancy neckwear
11 Stinging comment
12 Biblical "hairy one"
13 Like morning grass
22 Lacking slack
23 Fearsome dino
25 With 6-Down, Doctor Zhivago's portrayer
28 Boutonniere's place
29 "Little Women" sister
30 Western tribe
31 Cl⁻ or Na⁺
32 Lunar New Year
36 Watch spot
37 Évian, par exemple
38 Toward the stern
39 Mere pittance
40 Place to have a brioche
42 Do a cashier's job
43 "Geez Louise!"
44 Make a snarling sound
45 Pre-workout ritual
47 "Almost Paradise" author Susan
48 Some batteries
49 Kind of statement, to a programmer
50 Vegetarian's stipulation
51 Hotel bathroom amenities
54 Nobel city
55 Within a stone's throw
56 Great Lakes port
57 Sported
58 Got a move on
63 New Haven collegian

by Bruce Venzke and Stella Daily

24

ACROSS

1. Penny-pinch
6. Woes
10. Oats, to Trigger
14. "Deck the Halls," e.g.
15. Belle's gent
16. Auto shaft
17. Sex appeal
20. ___ judicata
21. Vintner's container
22. Some coffee orders
23. Amateur radioer
24. Initiation, e.g.
25. Where to grow carrots and spinach
33. Lycée, par exemple
34. Two cubed
35. Tool that's swung
36. It's typical
37. Anchor hoister
38. Scratch on a gem, e.g.
39. Bullring cheer
40. "Don't let these guys escape!"
41. Flinch or blink, say
42. Places to find some gems
45. "___ in China"
46. D-Day craft: Abbr.
47. Briny
50 & 52. Thomas Gainsborough portrait, with "The"
55. Game suggested by the first words of 17-, 25- and 42-Across
58. Super-duper
59. Continental coin
60. Go over, as lines
61. Latch (onto)
62. Aries or Libra
63. Flower with rays

DOWN

1. Memento of a knife fight
2. "Citizen ___"
3. Rainbow goddess
4. Soccer ___
5. Appease
6. Some early PCs
7. Unauthorized disclosure
8. Not keep up
9. Source of vitamin D
10. Not so slim
11. Sartre's "No ___"
12. If not
13. Clinton followers, for short
18. See 30-Down
19. Really bug
23. Place for a captain
24. Government in power
25. What a fang ejects
26. Worrisome food contamination
27. Charles who wrote "Winning Bridge Made Easy"
28. John, Paul, George or Ringo
29. Resided
30. With 18-Down, Tibetan V.I.P.
31. Meticulous
32. Brilliantly colored salamanders
37. Sharpshooters
38. Suffix with gab or song
40. Research money
41. ___ Stone (hieroglyphic key)
43. Rapper a k a Slim Shady
44. +
47. Men-only
48. Way off base?
49. Jay who does "Jaywalking"
50. One-horse town
51. Ponce de ___
52. Ferry or dinghy
53. Back then
54. Nieuwpoort's river
56. On the ___ vive
57. Form 1040 org.

by John Underwood

ACROSS
1 Catch on a ranch
6 Root beer brand
10 In
13 W.W. II conference site
14 Counterpart of lyrics
15 Ending with pay or plug
16 #1 hit
18 Brooch
19 Country's McEntire
20 Summer coolers
21 Comforting words
23 Magazine and newspaper revenue source
25 Larger-than-life
26 Some 1960s–'70s attire
31 Potpourri holder
35 Directional suffix
36 www page creation tool
37 English horn relatives
38 It can precede the starts of 16-, 26-, 43- and 58-Across and 10- and 33-Down
39 Muslim pilgrim's goal
40 Alan of "Betsy's Wedding"
41 Sunday offering: Abbr.
42 Faulty shot, as in tennis
43 Watch
46 Carter of "Gimme a Break!"
47 Spa treatment
52 Madrid museum
54 Not orig.
56 Middle name at Menlo Park
57 ___ shot (joke follow-up)
58 However
61 Rocks in a glass
62 Skyrockets
63 Prince's "Raspberry ___"
64 Deletes, with "out"
65 "That wasn't good!"
66 Dropped a line

DOWN
1 Stretchy synthetic
2 Sounded content
3 Hearty slices
4 Feedbag part
5 Feedbag morsel
6 Pull a fast one on
7 Egyptian slitherers
8 Casino cube
9 Actor's reading
10 Playground game
11 Mixed bag
12 Fail miserably
14 Strut on the runway
17 "Be silent," in scores
22 Worshipers' payments
24 Lincoln and Vigoda
25 Seeming eternity
27 '60s guru Timothy
28 Shiverer's sound
29 Start of the 22nd century
30 Strip under the mattress
31 Enjoy a tub
32 Up to the task
33 Manhattan Project and Operation Overlord
34 Piled up
38 Competition of sorts
39 Give a darn
41 NBC hit starting in '75
42 Yap, so to speak
44 Mourning of the N.B.A.
45 Sends out
48 Farm bundler
49 Bygone Olds
50 Cable box holder
51 Cause of sloppiness, maybe
52 ___ fixe
53 Paella need
54 Home ___
55 Staff note
59 "La-la" preceder
60 "Charlotte's Web" author's monogram

by Jim Hyres

ACROSS

1 "I'm glad that's over!"
5 "Green" sci.
9 Schindler of "Schindler's List"
14 Sound from a 57-Down
15 Writer Ephron
16 Like some Groucho Marx humor
17 Himalayan legend
18 Sketched
19 Speak histrionically
20 Revolve
23 "Honest!"
26 Put chips in a pot
27 "Don't miss the next episode . . ."
32 "Bye Bye Bye" boy band
33 Kind of sleep
34 Sleeping, say
36 Gave the thumbs-up
37 Start of many a pickup line
41 Tall tale
42 Cry
44 Luau serving
45 Set straight
47 Become a recluse, perhaps
51 Campaign fund-raising grp.
52 Rest stop features
53 Speaker of the catchphrase that starts 20-, 27- and 47-Across
58 Shade of green
59 Word with pepper or saw
60 Congregation's location
64 Signal to clear the road
65 Nat or Natalie

66 Hertz competitor
67 Courage
68 Give ___ to (approve)
69 Stun

DOWN

1 Like some humor
2 Weed whacker
3 Chow down
4 On paper
5 Evasive maneuver
6 Relative of a trumpet
7 Creme-filled snack
8 Croquet site
9 Act before the headliner
10 Indonesian island crossed by the Equator
11 The "K" in James K. Polk
12 Naysayer
13 Deli loaves
21 Robert of "Spenser: For Hire"
22 Weapon in 1940s headlines
23 Edward R. Murrow's "See ___"
24 Like a walrus
25 Talk show host Tom
28 Go around and around
29 ___ culpa
30 Do a favor
31 Pound, for example
35 Jobs for body shops
38 Geologic period
39 "___ and whose army?"

40 Arafat of the P.L.O.
43 Light muffin
46 Frog's perch
48 Inventor's goal
49 Verdi opera featuring "Ave Maria"
50 Gave birth in a stable
53 "Poppycock!"
54 Tennis's Nastase
55 Actress Sorvino
56 Org. that organizes camps
57 Big prowler
61 Longoria of "Desperate Housewives"
62 Diana Ross musical, with "The"
63 Dir. from Seattle to Las Vegas

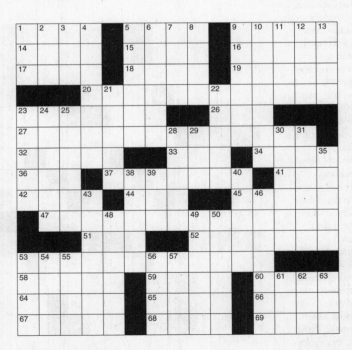

by Mike Nothnagel

ACROSS

1 "Madness" month
6 Crime-fighter Eliot Ness, notably
10 Hug givers
14 What a sun visor prevents
15 Saab or Subaru
16 Santa's "present" for a naughty child
17 Company that clears clogged drains
19 Game with Miss Scarlet and Professor Plum
20 "Faster!"
21 Spanish squiggle
22 Uses a stool
23 Phone part
25 Rocky hill
28 "___ on your life!"
29 Following
30 With 48-Across, popular computer product
32 Second Amendment rights org.
33 Adjective follower
36 Car for a star
37 Break, briefly . . . or a hint to this puzzle's theme
39 Use a keyboard
40 Held on to
41 Suffix with expert
42 Fancy tie
43 French political divisions
45 Barn bird
47 U.S.N.A. grad
48 See 30-Across
50 The Godfather's voice, e.g.
52 Put in ___ way
53 Scenic view
57 Greek Cupid
58 Friendly tournament format
60 Baseball's Matty or Felipe
61 Ladder step
62 1940s Bikini blast, in brief
63 Subject to mildew, perhaps
64 Web destination
65 Nick of "Lorenzo's Oil"

DOWN

1 Baseball team V.I.P.'s: Abbr.
2 Gobs
3 Assign an NC-17, e.g.
4 Corn and wheat
5 Nancy Drew or Joan of Arc
6 One who knows "the way"
7 Unlikely dog for a canine registry
8 Lunched, say
9 Neither's partner
10 Mishaps
11 Silver Cloud of autodom
12 Bea Arthur sitcom
13 Winter precipitation
18 Not fooled by
21 Explosive inits.
23 Steellike
24 Way off
25 Lecture
26 "Garfield" canine
27 Classic kids' show
31 Exhortation at a pub
32 SSW's opposite
34 Atop
35 New Jersey hoopsters
37 "Lovely ___, meter maid" (Beatles lyric)
38 Entry-level position: Abbr.
42 Ross Perot, in 1992 and 1996
44 Tummy muscles
45 Like pumpkins and traffic cones
46 Harry Potter prop
48 In front
49 Nurse Espinosa on "Scrubs"
51 Prefix with -plasm
53 Football kick
54 Cain's brother
55 Aerosol spray
56 Poker stake
58 Monopoly quartet: Abbr.
59 Pro vote in a French referendum

by Steve Kahn

28

ACROSS

1 Bird in the "Arabian Nights"
4 Traffic tie-up
9 Morning hour
14 Actor Gulager
15 Playful sprite
16 Throat dangler
17 Alphabetic trio
18 38-Across, in a sense
20 Decides one will
22 Afternoon social
23 Request to a switchboard oper.
24 Secular
25 Composer of the "Brandenburg Concertos," in brief
28 38-Across, in a sense
31 Throw out
35 Verdi aria
36 Squanders
38 1964 #1 hit by the Shangri-Las . . . or this puzzle's theme
42 Excite
43 Italian flowers
44 Mural site
45 38-Across, in a sense
49 Personify
52 Five-star
53 Letters before a pseudonym
56 U.R.L. ending
57 "Uncle" of old TV
59 38-Across, in a sense
63 Former Vladimir Putin org.
64 Zhou ___
65 Being of service
66 Funnyman Philips
67 Seat that may have a swivel top
68 All-night trucker's aid
69 Tibetan beast

DOWN

1 Soft drink since 1905
2 Friend since high school, say
3 Place for chalk
4 Petty quarrel
5 One-named singer for the 1960s Velvet Underground
6 Firefighter's tool
7 Resort city that shares its name with a Duran Duran hit
8 Did not disturb
9 Rapper Shakur
10 "Little" '60s singer
11 Hosiery shade
12 Third baseman Rodriguez
13 Schooner part
19 Pirate's domain
21 Plan
25 Mil. plane's boosted launch
26 Discarded: Var.
27 Setting for TV's "House"
29 War god on Olympus
30 Muddy area
32 Actress Hagen
33 Jiffy
34 "Naughty!"
36 Often-misused pronoun
37 Prefix with space
38 Murphy's is well known
39 Period to remember
40 Gmail alternative
41 Microscopic
45 Area connected to a kennel
46 Computer user's shortcut
47 Conundrum
48 Adidas competitor
50 It merged with Exxon
51 "What's shakin', ___?"
53 Skunk River city
54 Categorical imperative philosopher
55 Guthrie who sang about Alice
57 Opposite of bueno
58 "Mockingbird" singer Foxx, 1963
60 Southeast Asian language
61 Oklahoma native
62 Prefix with afternoon

by Barry C. Silk

ACROSS

1 Slightly
5 Got rid of a chaw
9 Perfume from petals
14 Formal fabric
15 Corrida creature
16 Pleasant Island, today
17 Kelly Clarkson or Taylor Hicks
18 Broadway's ___ Jay Lerner
19 Like unfortunate bullfighters
20 Stealing some computer memory?
23 Roll-call vote
24 Go off course
25 "Too bad!"
27 Squeegees' kin
30 Homework assignments
33 Stash away
34 Jackknife, for one
35 Tale of the gods
37 Stateside Ltd.
38 Narrow pieces
41 Kung fu star
42 Most of I-76 across Pennsylvania
44 Word of agreement
45 Lincoln Center offering
47 Beermat, e.g.
49 Drank slowly
50 Sig Chi, e.g.
51 Where Fermi went to university
52 Queasy
54 Always use the term "coloring agent"?
60 Sent out beams
62 Graph line
63 Tiger club
64 Where the action is
65 Bean town?
66 Maritime: Abbr.
67 Twangy
68 School in Berkshire, England
69 Sandwich from a sidewalk stand

DOWN

1 Found a perch
2 Vocal fanfare
3 Running ___
4 Come through
5 Puts on
6 Arctic
7 Djellaba wearer
8 "West Side Story" role
9 San ___, Tex.
10 Chinese cosmic order
11 Ways to make lefts and rights?
12 Realtor's calculation
13 Basketball's Tomjanovich
21 "Revenge of the ___"
22 Get to the point?
26 Outfielder's asset
27 Senate figure
28 Ancient Greek dialect
29 Assorted hydroxides?
30 Don or Lena
31 Square
32 Cordwood measure
34 Makeshift screwdriver
36 John, at sea
39 Coffeehouse order
40 "El Capitan" composer
43 Audio receiver
46 Saying grace
48 Huarache
49 Toyota rival
51 First-rate
52 Where Farsi is spoken
53 1965 Julie Christie role
55 Lowland
56 Take off
57 Sledge
58 Part of B.Y.O.B.
59 Inner, in combinations
61 Faline's mother, in "Bambi"

by Richard Silvestri

ACROSS

1 Footlong sandwiches
5 Lost traction
9 Post office purchase
14 Fairy tale meanie
15 Hatcher of "Lois & Clark"
16 Himalayan kingdom
17 Short on dough
19 Play a role none too subtly
20 Kind of paper for gift-wrapping
21 Short on dough
23 ___ to stern
25 Dedicatory verse
26 Sports org. for scholars
29 Finger food at a Spanish restaurant
32 Over-the-top review
36 The "A" in A/V
38 Howard Stern's medium
40 Tiny criticism to "pick"
41 Short on dough
44 Part of an iceberg that's visible
45 Sarge's superior
46 Aquafina competitor
47 Aardvark's fare
49 Attack en masse, as a castle
51 Architect Saarinen
52 ___ Beta Kappa
54 Individually
56 Short on dough
61 Bits of wisdom?
65 One washing down a driveway, e.g.
66 Short on dough
68 Eye-teasing paintings
69 Saskatchewan Indian
70 Teeny bit
71 See 22-Down
72 "Thundering" group
73 Agts. looking for tax cheats

DOWN

1 Downy
2 Wrinkly fruit
3 Garments that usually clasp in the back
4 Takes off on a cruise
5 Avenue
6 Fierce type, astrologically
7 Annoys
8 Jenny Craig regimen
9 Three-time P.G.A. champ
10 Word repeated after someone starts to show anger
11 Individually
12 Chess ending
13 Begged
18 ". . . and nothing ___"
22 With 71-Across, "White Men Can't Jump" co-star
24 Ballet's Fonteyn
26 Can./U.S./Mex. treaty
27 Give hints to
28 Good (at)
30 Barbecue area
31 Stick (to)
33 "___ Get Your Gun"
34 Church official
35 Prefix with -centric
37 Something good to strike
39 Unclose, poetically
42 Polite refusal
43 "Enough already!"
48 Globe
50 In an atlas, e.g.
53 #1 to Avis's #2
55 So-so grade
56 Restaurant acronym
57 "Uh-uh"
58 Nicholas I or II
59 Do art on glass, say
60 Partner of truth
62 "A ___ of One's Own"
63 Instrument that's plucked
64 Baseball's ___ the Man
67 Individually

by Harriet Clifton

ACROSS

1 Former U.N. chief Javier ___ de Cuéllar
6 Colorist
10 Black Power symbol
14 Site of Crockett's demise
15 Gutter site
16 Creep (along)
17 Spoonerism, usually
20 Something that may be brought back from the beach
21 Abbr. in a help wanted ad
22 Instruments played with bows
23 Sight along the Thames
28 Most acute
30 Bran material
31 Draft org.
32 Get on one's nerves
33 Indiana ___
35 Actress Roseanne
36 Word that can follow the starts of 17-, 23-, 51- and 59-Across
38 Clickable image
42 Baby screecher
44 Observe Yom Kippur
45 Deadly viper
48 "The Star-Spangled Banner" contraction
49 Like some dental floss
51 Hoedown folks
54 Author Vonnegut and others
55 General on a Chinese menu
56 Lilliputian
59 San Francisco tourist attraction
64 Modern ice cream flavor
65 Little explorer on Nickelodeon
66 Raise
67 Pete Rose's team
68 Small bit
69 Actress Moorehead

DOWN

1 Previous
2 Singer Fitzgerald
3 Slickers and the like
4 Akihito's title: Abbr.
5 Madhouse
6 Abhor
7 Popular e-mail provider
8 Grandmother of Enoch
9 Abbr. after some generals' names
10 That's all
11 Metal bars
12 Crews' craft
13 Postdocs often publish them
18 Gangsters' foes
19 Elliptical
24 Emcee's delivery
25 Word between two last names
26 Etymological basis
27 Axes
28 Putin's former org.
29 Pitcher's stat
33 Small bit
34 Instrument often accompanied by a pair of small drums
36 Swiss painter Paul
37 "Happy Days" put-down
39 Crew's leader
40 Atomic number of hydrogen
41 Flanders of "The Simpsons"
43 "It's ___ than that!"
44 Great reverence
45 Request
46 Future knight
47 Puckered
49 Open, in a way
50 Cpls. and others
52 One of the Three Musketeers
53 Centipede maker
57 Gaelic language
58 Newts
60 Tpkes.
61 Back-to-school time: Abbr.
62 "Huh?"
63 Big bike

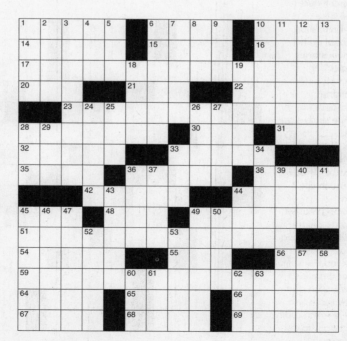

by Jonathan Gersch

ACROSS

1 Classic muscle cars
5 Stellar bear
9 Not be able to take
14 Juillet's follower
15 Gad about
16 Valuable find
17 Scrap the original strategy
19 Party spreads
20 Bikini, for one
21 Part of a suit
23 Rap's Dr. ___
24 Big spread
26 Mrs., in Madrid
27 ___ Mae (Whoopi's "Ghost" role)
28 Broke ground
30 Loop looper
33 Restrained
35 Chapel fixture
36 Three-time 60-homer man
37 Personal quirk
39 Anthem starter
43 Bandleader Eubanks, familiarly
46 Metropolis figure
49 Muscle shirt, e.g.
53 Rock's ___ Lonely Boys
54 Pewter component
55 Glass of "This American Life"
56 Lock
58 Common Market inits.
59 Cyclist Armstrong
61 "Cool!"
64 Unaided
66 What the ends of 17-, 30-, and 49-Across spell
68 Comic Amsterdam
69 Pandora's boxful
70 Cry after the sound of a bell

71 Dag Hammarskjöld, for one
72 Cry after the sound of a bell
73 PC suite components

DOWN

1 Totally smitten
2 Attention-getting sound
3 On empty
4 Took off with
5 Location to bookmark: Abbr.
6 Driver's license prerequisite
7 All there
8 Plot feature in many a western
9 Calm
10 Support, of a sort
11 Ballpark buy
12 Take too far
13 Use again, as a Ziploc bag
18 Catcher's place
22 Blood's rival
25 ___ Na Na
28 & 29 Numbers that add to tres
29 See 28-Down
31 Big copper exporter
32 Wanted G.I.
34 One of 10,000 in Minnesota
38 "Who's on first?" asker
40 Spicy bowlful
41 2007, por ejemplo
42 What a nod may mean
44 Curse, of sorts

45 Designer Wang
47 Neighbor of Leb.
48 Gregg pro
49 Cooks, in a way
50 Stay out of sight
51 Call for more
52 "The Blues Brothers" director John
57 Mattress giant
60 Knick rival
62 Fill-in
63 Bauxite and others
65 Prof. Brainard of "The Absent-Minded Professor"
67 AOL, e.g.

by Curtis Yee

ACROSS

1 #1 number two who became the #2 number one
6 Actors who mug
10 Talking equine of '60s TV
14 Roll over, as a subscription
15 Neighbor of Yemen
16 Toy on a string
17 Food from heaven
18 Lot in life
19 ___-again (like some Christians)
20 She offered Excalibur to the future King Arthur
23 Garment accompanying a girdle
24 Last letter, in London
25 Gordon of "Oklahoma!"
29 Went out, as a fire
31 Club discussed in clubhouses: Abbr.
34 Guiding philosophy
35 Couch
36 Standard
37 Popular canned tuna
40 Word of invitation
41 Broadway award
42 Alleviates
43 Nile stinger
44 Hockey legend Gordie
45 Handles the food for the party
46 Big bird of the outback
47 Quilt locale
48 Columbia, in an old patriotic song
55 Witty Ephron
56 Lamb : ewe :: ___ : mare

57 Ram, astrologically
59 Voting no
60 Warren of the Supreme Court
61 Do, as a puzzle
62 Something to slip on?
63 Whirling current
64 County ENE of London

DOWN

1 Elbow's place
2 "Are we agreed?"
3 Late celebrity ___ Nicole Smith
4 Repair
5 Sag on a nag
6 Labor leader Jimmy who mysteriously disappeared
7 Amo, amas, ___ . . .

8 Trig or geometry
9 Take lightly
10 "Oops! I made a mistake"
11 Castle, in chess
12 "Jane ___"
13 "___ we now our gay apparel"
21 Valuable rock
22 ___ Zeppelin
25 Holy city of Islam
26 One of the Three Musketeers
27 Cheeta, in "Tarzan" films
28 Serving with chop suey
29 "Lorna ___"
30 Questionable
31 Rapper's entourage
32 Garson of "Mrs. Miniver"
33 Accumulate

35 The white in a whiteout
36 Tidy
38 Crayfish dish
39 One who could use a shrink
44 Medical care grp.
45 Corporate V.I.P.
46 EarthLink transmission
47 Stomach
48 Disappeared
49 Old Harper's Bazaar artist
50 Wart causer, in legend
51 Rocklike
52 Greek love god
53 Needs medicine
54 Campbell of "Scream"
55 40 winks
58 Topic for Dr. Ruth

by Randall J. Hartman

34

ACROSS

1 The gamut
5 Places to kick habits
11 Merino mother
14 Comic Chappelle
15 Like a paradise
16 Gen ___
17 Cool treats
18 Wildlife manager
20 Home of Smith College
22 Like some heirs
23 Flop or lop follower
26 100 square meters
29 Home of the U.S. Military Academy
33 Run out
35 Like a greenhorn
36 Start the kitty
37 Suffix with psych-
38 Leopold Bloom's creator
40 Maryland collegian
41 Unicorn in a 1998 movie
42 Words of commitment
43 Correo ___ (words on an envelope)
44 Home of Notre Dame
48 In position
49 "Blame It ___" (Michael Caine film)
50 Most-cooked parts of roasts
52 Home of Michigan State
59 Sites for stargazers
61 With 64-Across, 2005 Charlize Theron title role
62 Author Rand
63 Way past ripe
64 See 61-Across

65 "Absolutely!"
66 Ball
67 Puts into play

DOWN

1 Score after deuce
2 Food in a shell
3 [see other side]
4 Citrus peels
5 Wine and dine
6 Mingo player on "Daniel Boone"
7 Source of hashish
8 Work without ___
9 Steven ___, real-life subject of the 1987 film "Cry Freedom"
10 Act starter
11 Former lovers, e.g.
12 Minuscule
13 Mess up

19 Flow out
21 "The Battle Hymn of the Republic" writer
24 It may come with more than one side
25 Colorist's vessel
26 "The Tempest" king
27 Mete out
28 Devotees of fine dining
30 Test for fit
31 ___-Man
32 Have a tab
34 Nova ___
38 Triangular sail
39 Lyric poem
43 "The King ___"
45 Boorish sorts, in Canada
46 Naysayer

47 Ready for the rubber room
51 Major mess
53 Sporty auto roof
54 Plasterer's strip
55 Johnson of "Laugh-In"
56 Salon goos
57 Pouting look
58 "Need You Tonight" band
59 Compensation
60 Caustic alkali

by John Underwood

ACROSS

1 With 1-Down, 1982 Richard Pryor/Jackie Gleason film
4 Half court game?
7 Part of an auto accident
13 Crude structure?
15 Tourist's aid
16 "Understood!"
17 Like a band of Amazons
18 Iran-Contra grp.
19 Draftsman's tool (and a hint to this puzzle's theme)
20 Satchel in the Hall of Fame
23 Little squirt
24 Poli ___
25 Aunt of Prince Harry
26 Dogma
28 Conclusion, in Germany
31 Levy on a 33-Across
33 Place to build
35 63-Across, in Málaga
36 Like vinegar
37 Cookout sites
39 Foundation exec.
40 Frank McCourt memoir
42 A few
43 Suffix with exist
45 Means of fortunetelling
47 ___ account (never)
48 "___ got it!"
50 King in a celebrated 1970s U.S. tour
51 Clampett player
52 Attend to the final detail
54 Crimson foe

55 Commits to, as an interest rate
56 Ferris in film
60 Intent, as a listener
61 Field of unknowns?
62 Hand-color, in a way
63 Rotation period
64 Muesli morsel

DOWN

1 See 1-Across
2 Shake a leg
3 Old N.Y.C. lines
4 Title guy in a 1980 Carly Simon hit
5 A Waugh
6 Any part of Polynésie
7 Where Mosul is
8 Waiter's armload
9 Guard's workplace

10 Iroquois and others
11 Grammar concern
12 Plays a campus prank on, informally
14 Gridiron formation
15 Dutch beer brand
19 Big load
20 1974 Medicine Nobelist George ___
21 Bayer alternative
22 Influential group
23 Singing Ritter
26 Implied
27 Go ___ (deteriorate)
29 Quints' name
30 Hardly strict with
32 Relative of a chickadee

34 Fashion a doily
38 Big name in cellular service
41 "___ Cheerleaders" (1977 film)
42 "I'm kidding!"
44 Brought forth
46 Endless 9-to-5 job, e.g.
49 Op-ed, typically
51 Poem of lament
52 E. ___
53 What to call a king
54 Faulkner's ___ Varner
55 Iron pumper's muscle
56 No longer edible
57 Wall St. action
58 Diamond stat
59 Disloyal sort

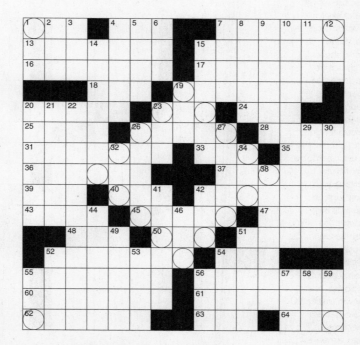

by Bonnie L. Gentry and Victor Fleming

ACROSS

1 "Get out of here!"
5 Scott who draws "Dilbert"
10 Heart problem
14 Tortoise's race opponent
15 Argue against
16 Attempt at a basket
17 Fe, chemically
18 Actress Verdugo
19 Loving strokes
20 Course option
23 Hold the wheel
24 "___ So Fine," #1 Chiffons hit
25 Double curve
28 Old photo shade
32 Space cut by a scythe
34 ___ Khan
37 Response option
40 Ballet skirt
42 Dweller along the Volga
43 Signal hello or goodbye
44 Electric light option
47 Hedge plant
48 Person under 21
49 Group singing "Hallelujah!"
51 Sault ___ Marie
52 Stout drink
55 Parts to play
59 Quiz option
64 Advertising award
66 "Praise be to ___"
67 Lhasa ___
68 Easter servings
69 String bean's opposite
70 Person under 20
71 Optometrists' concerns
72 Department of ___
73 Ocean eagle

DOWN

1 Freighters, e.g.
2 Diamond weight
3 Came up
4 Tightens, with "up"
5 Space
6 Place to get an egg salad sandwich
7 Eve's second son
8 Chew (on)
9 Old hat
10 Nile nippers
11 Shoo off
12 Mouth-burning
13 Travelers from another galaxy, for short
21 Glenn of the Eagles
22 Professional grp.
26 Comedian Martin
27 "The Taming of the ___"
29 Consumers of Purina and Iams food
30 Vidi in "Veni, vidi, vici"
31 Playful trick
33 Opposite ENE
34 They're smashed in a smasher
35 "Go fast!," to a driver
36 Back then
38 Courtroom affirmation
39 Western U.S. gas giant
41 Carrier of 13-Down
45 Berlin Mrs.
46 Take on, as employees
50 Spin
53 Pages (through)
54 Key of Mozart's Symphony No. 39
56 Outcast
57 Ruhr Valley city
58 Gem
60 One of TV's "Friends"
61 ___ Vista (search engine)
62 Final
63 Mule or clog
64 Revolutionary Guevara
65 Make, as a wager

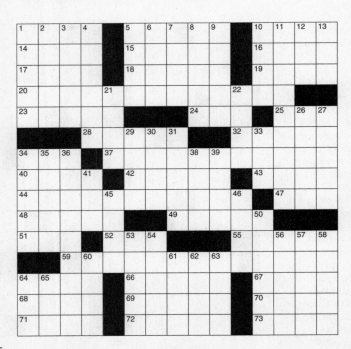

by Kurt Mengel and Jan-Michele Gianette

ACROSS

1 Director Kazan
5 Singer Lane of old TV
9 Challenge in a western
13 Artist Chagall
14 Developer's land
16 A pop
17 Computer introduced by Steve Jobs
18 ___ dish (lab item)
19 Full of pep
20 First showing at an all-day film festival? (1988)
23 Genetic material
24 Prankster's bit
25 Second showing (1970)
34 First sign, astrologically
35 Crystal-lined rock
36 Rocky peak
37 Highland headgear
38 Paycheck booster
39 Packed away
40 Greek H
41 Von Richthofen's title
42 Disloyal
44 Third showing (1975)
47 Taking after
48 Motorists' org.
49 Final showing (2004)
57 Graph line
58 Wipe clean
59 The Hawkeyes of college sports
60 Beanery handout
61 Hearing-related
62 "Beg pardon . . ."

63 Mideast's Gulf of ___
64 Avian sources of red meat
65 Ticked off

DOWN

1 Send out
2 Poor, as excuses go
3 It includes Mesopotamia
4 Damn
5 Having fun
6 La ___ Tar Pits
7 Upside-down sleepers
8 Neutral shade
9 Create fashions
10 Speaks ill of
11 Plot unit
12 Tot's repeated query

15 Self-important sorts
21 Printers' supplies
22 Red in the middle
25 Assigned stars to
26 Muse with a lyre
27 Joltin' Joe
28 Ancient marketplace
29 A little before the hour
30 Climb onto
31 Novelist Calvino
32 "That's a lie!"
33 Eco-friendly
38 San Francisco and environs
41 Place for a hayfork

42 Herr's mate
43 Biblical liar
45 Nissan, once
46 Atelier sights
49 Pink-slipped
50 Speeder's risk
51 Loyal
52 Damage
53 Biblical twin
54 Gallery-filled part of the Big Apple
55 Basin accompanier
56 Unlikely to bite
57 Physicians' grp.

by Ray Fontenot

ACROSS

1 Great Trek participant of the 1830s
5 Courtroom fig.
11 Bake sale grp.
14 Bowed, in music
15 "Yippee!"
16 Alley ___
17 Newts and such
19 "The Addams Family" cousin
20 Nocturnal beetle
21 Sugar suffix
22 ___ equal footing
23 Senior Saarinen
24 Take apart
26 Setting for a chaise longue
28 In groups
29 Deflating sound
30 When repeated, part of a Beatles refrain
33 Services' partner
34 Go-between, and a clue to 17-, 24-, 49- and 57-Across
37 Prized violin, briefly
40 Canned fare since 1937
41 Univ. staffers
44 School papers
46 Downsize, maybe
49 Salon job
52 ___ Potti
53 Totally confused
54 In the style of
55 Hit close to home?
56 Kick ___ storm
57 Locale of Uhuru Peak
59 Israeli airport city
60 Lover of Cesario, in "Twelfth Night"
61 Neighbor of Wash.

62 City grid: Abbr.
63 Take stock of
64 Features of greenhouses

DOWN

1 Stout-legged hounds
2 Sources of wisdom
3 Bakery treats
4 Lion, for one
5 Ill-fated captain
6 Trinity member
7 "Me too"
8 Long lock
9 Risktaker's challenge
10 "I see" sounds
11 Indicate, in a way
12 Came to

13 Suitability
18 Actress Powers of "Cyrano de Bergerac"
22 Something to cry over?
24 Knight's list
25 Bit of plankton
27 Dancer Charisse
31 Eiger, for one
32 Soul mate?
34 "___ mia!"
35 It pops into the head
36 Tussaud's title: Abbr.
37 Wren's cathedral
38 X marks it
39 Double-checks
41 Rarer than rare
42 Took in, perhaps
43 Old salts
45 Garden pests

47 Worked like Rumpelstiltskin
48 Swindler's work
50 ___ Island (museum site)
51 Dewy-eyed
55 Lambs' laments
57 R.V. hookup provider
58 Wrong start?

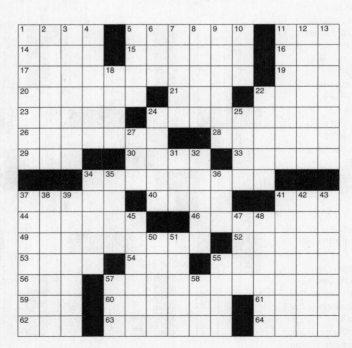

by Barbara Olson

ACROSS

1 Gem units
7 Revolutionary Guevara
10 Sea creature that moves sideways
14 Common recipe amount
15 Actor Holbrook
16 Turner of Hollywood
17 Masonry work that may be smoothed with a trowel
19 Grace finisher
20 Deadly snake
21 Shoving away, football-style
23 Director Bob who won a Tony, Oscar and Emmy all in the same year
24 Evicts
25 Quester for the Golden Fleece
28 Hen's place
30 "It's a sin to tell ___"
31 Goes 80, say
34 Fellow
37 More rain and less light, e.g., to a pilot
40 Sault ___ Marie
41 Ill-___ gains
42 Hitchhiker's need
43 Tabbies
44 Person whose name appears on a museum plaque, e.g.
45 Zorro's weapon
48 Colorado resort
51 Some memorization in arithmetic class
54 Airport overseer: Abbr.
57 Director Kazan
58 Earlier . . . or a hint to the words circled in 17-, 21-, 37- and 51-Across

60 Book after John
61 Coach Parseghian
62 White fur
63 Two tablets every six hours, e.g.
64 Thieve
65 Target and J. C. Penney

DOWN

1 ___ Nostra
2 Six-legged intruders
3 Sign on, as for another tour of duty
4 N.C. State's group
5 University of Arizona's home
6 Leopard markings
7 Rub raw
8 .5
9 Singer Fitzgerald
10 Zip one's lip
11 Harold who directed "Groundhog Day"
12 Concerning
13 Hair over the forehead
18 State known for its cheese: Abbr.
22 Hen's place
23 Enemies
25 1975 thriller that took a big bite at the box office
26 Very much
27 Father
28 Give
29 Chief Norse god
31 Many a person whose name starts Mac
32 Flower holders
33 Suffix with differ
34 Enter
35 Ruin

36 Belgian river to the North Sea
38 "Zounds!"
39 Laundry implement that might make a 43-Down
43 See 39-Down
44 Gobi or Mojave
45 Lieu
46 Radio word after "Roger"
47 Skips
48 Popular BBC import, for short
49 ___-mo replay
50 Israel's Shimon
52 Skier's transport
53 Prefix with -nautic
54 Light-skinned
55 Actress Heche
56 Citrus coolers
59 M.D.'s group

by Peter A. Collins

ACROSS

1 It's a no-no
6 Up for it
10 Hook attachment
14 Shia's deity
15 Letter-shaped beam
16 Long ago
17 Colorful food fish
18 Kid around
19 Mix up
20 Deeply hurt
23 Benevolent fellow
25 Poem of exaltation
26 Quitter's cry
27 Abs strengtheners
29 Big bash
32 Partner of poivre
33 Ark complement
34 Checks for errors
36 Ramadan observance
41 Be testy with
42 Pride member
44 Little terror
47 Genesis garden
48 Attached, in a way
50 Racial equality org.
52 Whale group
53 Suffix with butyl
54 Gulliver's creator
59 Mineralogists' samples
60 Met solo
61 Game played on a wall
64 Scot's attire
65 Took a turn
66 Like leprechauns
67 To be, to Brutus
68 Scots' turndowns
69 Conical dwelling

DOWN

1 "___ Te Ching"
2 Yodeler's setting
3 Semiformal
4 Pearl Harbor site
5 "Come on, that's enough!"
6 Doll for boys
7 Help in wrongdoing
8 Kind of note
9 Art Deco notable
10 Petty officer
11 Class clown's doings
12 Yule tree hanging
13 Pulitzer winner Studs
21 N.F.L. six-pointers
22 Drink heartily
23 "I know what you're thinking" ability
24 Fish story teller
28 www addresses
29 Wordless "Ouch!"
30 Summer month, in Paris
31 Rock's ___ Lobos
34 Sherlock Holmes prop
35 Red tag event
37 Klutzy
38 ___ about (rove)
39 Excursion diversion
40 Cel character
43 S.F.-to-Spokane direction
44 Bit of humor most people can't get
45 Native New Zealanders
46 Discussion groups
48 Wrecker's job
49 "Finally finished!"
51 Social stratum
52 Jr.-year exams
55 Goldie of "Laugh-In"
56 General vicinity
57 Punch-in time for many
58 MetroCard cost
62 "The Waste Land" monogram
63 ___-crab soup

by Norma Johnson

When this puzzle has been completed, shade in the letters of 35-Across everywhere they appear in the grid, revealing three letters and three lines.

ACROSS

1 Karate blow
5 Winkler role, with "the"
9 Cartoon pics
13 Wertmüller who directed "Seven Beauties"
14 "___ Gold"
16 Sky lights?
17 Brewery fixture
18 Knocking sound
20 Solid alcohol
22 All you need, in a Beatles song
23 Have a TV dinner, say
24 Fire sign?
26 Late singer Rawls
29 Classic Mercedes-Benz roadsters
30 Homes that may have circular drives
32 Long, long time
33 Soviet labor camp
34 Automaker Ferrari
35 July 4th message to America
40 Theological schools: Abbr.
41 Buys for brew lovers
42 Grand ___ Opry
43 How many teens go to movies
46 Not many
49 160, once
50 Mentholated cigarettes
51 Gawk (at)
53 Brief moments
54 Regains one's senses, with "up"
55 Memorable title film role of 1971
60 Some nest eggs, for short
61 Risk-taking Knievel

62 Prod
63 ___-Rooter
64 Old comics boy
65 Those, to Carlos
66 Official with a list

DOWN

1 Shutters
2 Having a gap
3 Initiations
4 "Gloria ___" (hymn start)
5 Roll up
6 Suffix with pay
7 Web
8 Fanatic
9 Adorable
10 Pond denizen
11 Mauna ___
12 Sound barrier breaker: Abbr.
15 Tend the hearth

19 Greetings of long ago
21 Early Ping-Pong score
24 Puncture
25 Enchanting
26 Horne who sang "Stormy Weather"
27 Like mud
28 3–2, en español
31 Cunning
33 Some docs
34 Masthead names, for short
35 "War is ___"
36 Green card?
37 "Phooey!"
38 Lao-___
39 "___ Fine" (1963 Chiffons hit)
40 Assn.
43 ___-doke
44 Opposite of dia

45 Medicinal amount
46 Denmark's ___ Islands
47 Mistakes
48 Big name in oil
52 Snazzy Ford debut of 1955
53 Capital of Manche
54 Dict. offerings
55 Opium ___
56 Correct ending?
57 Part of a sleep cycle
58 Some football linemen: Abbr.
59 Down Under hopper

by Patrick Blindauer

ACROSS

1 Warm-blooded animal
7 Polite concurrence
14 Neighbor of Sudan
16 Behind on payments, after "in"
17 Five-pointed ocean denizen
18 Short sleeps
19 Charged particles
20 1950s Wimbledon champ Lew
21 Singer Morissette
24 Justice div. that conducts raids
25 And so on: Abbr.
28 Pepsi and RC
29 Viewer-supported TV network
30 Sag
32 E. ___ (health menace)
33 Help
34 Sportscaster Howard
35 Opposite WSW
36 Creature suggested by this puzzle's circled letters
38 ___ v. Wade
39 Criticize in a petty way
41 Cleaning tool in a bucket
42 Turner who sang "Proud Mary"
43 ___ firma
44 ___ Bartlet, president on "The West Wing"
45 Trigonometric ratios
46 Michigan's ___ Canals
47 Sn, in chemistry
48 Unpaired
49 Threadbare
51 "What were ___ thinking?"
52 Driver's levy
55 Drinkers may run them up
59 Kansas expanse
60 Back: Fr.
61 Coarse-haired burrowers
62 2001 Sean Penn film

DOWN

1 Enero or febrero
2 "You ___ here"
3 "Mamma ___!"
4 Where Moses got the Ten Commandments
5 Stella ___ (Belgian beer)
6 Tilts
7 Regatta boats
8 ___ Good Feelings
9 Spanish Mlle.
10 Darners
11 Tiny battery type
12 Dadaist Jean
13 Editor's work: Abbr.
15 ___ poetica
21 One of two in "résumé"
22 Cuckoos
23 Fast, in music
24 Body's midsection
26 Jewelry for a sandal wearer
27 Rank below brigadier general
29 Cherry seed
30 Uno y uno
31 "The magic word"
33 1 or 11, in blackjack
34 Saucer's go-with
36 Suffix with pay
37 Pea's home
40 Fade
42 "Tip-Toe Thru' the Tulips" singer
44 They cause bad luck
45 ___ Mist (7 Up competitor)
47 Characteristic
48 Puppeteer Lewis
50 Other, south of the border
51 Abbr. in TV listings
52 Tach measure, for short
53 ". . . man ___ mouse?"
54 River to the Rhine
56 D.D.E. defeated him
57 Playtex item
58 Half a year of coll.

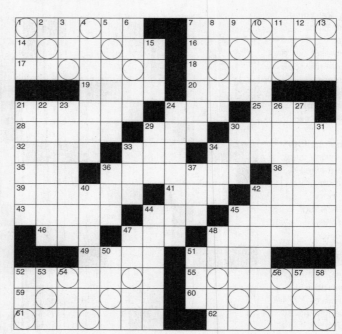

by Peter A. Collins

ACROSS
1 Completely wreck
6 Pipe shape
9 Twin Falls's home
14 High home
15 Finder's reward
16 Generous soul
17 Loan to a
company
before it goes
public, say
20 Computer
command
after cut
21 Gill opening
22 D.C. insider
24 N.F.L. position:
Abbr.
26 Lake that is a
source of the
Mississippi
30 Spilling out
34 Director
Browning
35 Russian country
house
36 Slangy turndown
37 History chapters
38 Periods of unrest
42 Life stories
43 Unedited
44 South Beach
plan and others
46 Seating info
47 Remover of
impurities
50 "___ Song" (John
Denver tune)
52 ___ one-eighty
53 Mormons, initially
54 Crash-probing
agcy.
56 Place to shop in
Tokyo
59 The starts to
17-, 30-, 38-
and 47-Across,
collectively
65 Arboreal Aussie
66 Be short
67 Pour out from

68 On the tail of
69 Ernie of golf
70 Social level

DOWN
1 Treater's pickup
2 "___ the land
of the free . . ."
3 Racing feat
4 Broadway
musical with
the song "The
Gods Love
Nubia"
5 Crab morsels
6 Lacking vigor
7 Handout at
a tiki bar
8 Shutterbug's
purchase
9 Set off
10 Formal rulings
11 Bird: Prefix

12 Old biddy
13 .com alternative
18 Impress clearly
19 Land (on)
22 Part of a
commercial
name after "i"
23 It may be standing
25 Extended, as
a membership
27 Lights on posts,
perhaps
28 Didn't work that
hard
29 They may pop
up nowadays
31 Greek R's
32 Greek T
33 Nascar ___
37 Expressionist
Nolde
39 Harsh and
metallic

40 Long. crosser
41 ___ Amin
42 It has a supporting
role
45 Grads-to-be: Abbr.
47 Home mixologist's
spot
48 ___ gallery
49 Go bankrupt
51 Fireplace
55 Fraternal org.
57 Tiny fraction
of a min.
58 Coors brand
59 Calypso cousin
60 Punch-in-the-gut
response
61 Rebellious Turner
62 Saddler's tool
63 Baseball's Master
Melvin
64 Carrie of
"Creepshow"

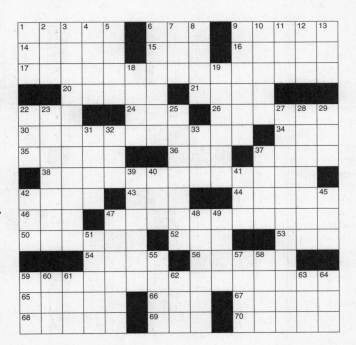

by Pete Muller

ACROSS

1 SeaWorld attractions
6 50 Cent piece
9 Constantly change lanes
14 "Peachy!"
15 Voters liked him twice
16 Stan's partner in old films
17 Poke, in a way
18 Mature before being picked
20 Sport played on the first word of its name
22 Ax user, e.g.
23 Page turner
28 Eerie
29 Tot's wheels
32 Say "uncle"
33 Popular clog-buster
34 California's state bird
35 Sport played in the first word of its name
39 Gucci competitor
40 Scrabble draw
41 Prefix with -gon
42 The lion in "The Lion, the Witch and the Wardrobe"
43 Go out, as embers
46 Organized crime
48 "You can come out now"
51 Sport played on the first word of its name
54 It may get stuck in a movie theater
58 Home of Brigham Young University
59 Fictional Scarlett
60 Lead-in to many a chef's name
61 Fan's opposite

62 "Shucks!"
63 Horse color
64 Alley pickup

DOWN

1 Boxing combo
2 Installed anew, as flooring
3 Took a taxi, with "it"
4 Ringlike island
5 Scattered over the earth
6 They run rapids
7 Related
8 William for whom a colony was named
9 Not as good
10 Inventor Whitney

11 European peak
12 Compete
13 Poetic darkness
19 Limerick's home
21 Neon ___ (fish)
24 Contents of una fontana
25 Use a rotary phone
26 Dr. ___ of "Austin Powers" films
27 Divinity sch. subject
30 How sardines are often packed
31 Pitcher who says "Oh, yeaahh!"
33 Crime lab evidence
34 Some hikers' targets, for short
35 St. Louis attraction
36 Appraise

37 Noted cheese town
38 Tither's amount
39 Poker payoff
42 Irish Rose's beau
43 Some Plains Indians
44 "Should that come to pass"
45 Pooh's mopey pal
47 Words after court or rule
49 Frosh, next year
50 Consign to the junkyard
52 "Yikes!"
53 Corker
54 Conk
55 Dull responses
56 Cry from Scrooge
57 Strapped wear

by Patrick Merrell

ACROSS

1 Cutlass or 88, in the auto world
5 Result of a serious head injury
9 Refrigerates
14 Hilarious happening
15 Not new
16 Big foil maker
17 *It rolls across the Plains
19 Poverty-stricken
20 Church music maker
21 Bean from which sauce is made
23 18, e.g., as a minimum for voting
24 When repeated, a Hawaiian fish
27 Kevin of "Field of Dreams"
29 Psychiatrists' appointments
33 Western Indians
34 First responder, say: Abbr.
35 ESE's reverse
36 Spoke roughly
39 Former coin in the Trevi Fountain
41 Barely chewable
43 "It is so"
44 California city on a bay, slangily
46 Shooters' org.
47 Coach Parseghian
48 Edith who sang "La Vie en Rose"
49 Responsible for, as something bad
52 Wife of Marc Antony
55 Vivacity
56 "The Tell-Tale Heart" teller
57 1967 Montreal attraction
59 Saint ___, Caribbean nation

63 Range maker
65 *Beehive contents
68 Put back to 0000, say
69 Preppy shirt label
70 Jai ___
71 Birch and larch
72 Politicos with a donkey symbol
73 Barber's call

DOWN

1 Roughly
2 False witness
3 Rapper Snoop ___
4 Really ticks off
5 Snarling dog
6 The Buckeyes, for short
7 Result of a ransacking
8 Like some committees

9 Card game with melding
10 Bullfight cry
11 *Juice drink brand
12 Where Moose meet
13 Follower of nay or sooth
18 ___ B'rith
22 & 25 What the ends of the answers to the four starred clues are examples of
26 ___ way, shape or form
28 Try out
29 ___-help
30 Mideast leader
31 *Alluring dance
32 Moved like a pendulum

37 Coin across the Atlantic
38 Unhearing
40 Land east of the Urals
42 Eats
45 Cautions
50 Easter bloom
51 Big-billed bird
52 Bedazzling museum works
53 Person who shows promise
54 Green garden bug
58 Seep
60 ___ slaw
61 Large-screen cinema format
62 Not much
64 Maiden name preceder
66 ___ de plume
67 Mag. staffers

by Elizabeth A. Long

ACROSS

1 Rocker Ocasek
4 "American Pie" beauty
9 Window area
13 Sufficient, old-style
15 Walt Whitman's "___ the Body Electric"
16 Far from harbor
17 *1942 film with the line "What makes saloonkeepers so snobbish?"
19 Look inside?
20 Prefix with mural
21 Long-distance letters
23 Commercials
24 *Bench sharer
28 One with fingers crossed
30 Lead-in to while
31 "Illmatic" rapper
32 Like a clock that has hands
34 Ensembles of eight
37 You might crack one while playing
38 Word before pool or park
41 *Japanese grill
43 "Get it?"
44 "Me, Myself & ___," 2000 Jim Carrey film
46 Peter of "Goodbye, Mr. Chips"
48 When Alexander Hamilton and Aaron Burr dueled
50 Goof
51 Letters
55 Actor Milo
56 *Underwater creature whose males give birth
58 "Finger-lickin' good" restaurant
59 Fort ___, N.J.
61 Had dinner at home
62 Not at home

64 How the answer to each of the nine starred clues repeats
68 Barely cooked
69 Bor-r-ring voice
70 Alternative to truth in a party game
71 Uno+uno+uno
72 The "S" in WASP
73 "Help!"

DOWN

1 Say, as a pledge
2 More ludicrous
3 Sportscaster Bob
4 Nothing
5 Blind ___ bat
6 Clamor
7 Old llama herder
8 Christie who created Hercule Poirot
9 Instrument that wails
10 *They live on acres of Acre's
11 *Rick Blaine in 17-Across, e.g.
12 Sets (down)
14 Start liking
18 "Kapow!"
22 Throat part
25 "Nay" sayer
26 Popular aerobic program
27 *Many-acred homes
29 Bobby's wife on "Dallas"
33 "Well, that beats all!"
35 Bawled (out)
36 It might need to be settled
38 Secretive org.
39 *Classic Chinese military treatise, with "The"

40 *Fearful 1917–20 period
42 Bar mitzvah dance
45 Slangy denial
47 Hammed it up
49 River nymphs, in Greek myth
52 Basketball venues
53 San ___, Argentina
54 Camera eyes
57 Derisive laugh
58 Mario ___, Nintendo racing game
60 More, in commercialese
63 Verbal nod
65 Be a pugilist
66 Plastic ___ Band
67 Evening hour

by Natan Last

ACROSS

1 Example of 41-Across
7 Example of 41-Across
15 Like "Survivor" groups
16 "That's fine"
17 ___ Quimby of children's books
18 Most finicky
19 Not fighting
21 Squeezed (out)
22 Ballerina's digit
23 Suffix with racket or rocket
25 Weakens, as support
29 Line up
32 Push (for)
36 Needle part
37 Mauna ___
39 Example of 41-Across
41 Theme of this puzzle
45 Example of 41-Across
46 90 degree pipe joint
47 Result of getting worked up
48 Call the whole thing off
50 On the wagon
54 Eton students, e.g.
56 Symbol of sturdiness
58 City map abbr.
59 Tacks on
63 Works of Swift and Wilde
66 They're over the hill
70 Dancing locale
71 "Be delighted"
72 Low tie
73 Example of 41-Across
74 Example of 41-Across

DOWN

1 Rock bands?
2 Keynote speaker, e.g.
3 Less firm
4 Instrument with a conical bore
5 Sha follower
6 French ice cream
7 Bush league?: Abbr.
8 Merle Haggard, self-descriptively
9 Sail a zigzag course
10 Little one
11 Put up with
12 Bread for a Reuben
13 Speakers' no-nos
14 Amount left after all is said and done
20 Unagi, at a sushi restaurant
24 Actress Dawson of "Rent"
26 Polar denizen
27 Polar explorer
28 Salty septet
30 Therapeutic plant
31 "___ got mail"
33 Humanities degs.
34 Memory unit
35 Cries from the woods
38 "I love him like ___"
40 Defendant's plea, informally
41 Not work out
42 Kirlian photography image
43 Four-footed TV star
44 Jar part
49 Thank-yous along the Thames
51 Black Russians may go on it
52 ___ Brothers
53 Fix, as a shoe
55 Buffalo hockey player
57 Barbecue offering
60 Bug juice?
61 Like Radio City Music Hall, informally
62 Hitch
64 Pint-size
65 "Mm-hmm"
66 Chart topper
67 "Do ___ do"
68 It may be tidy
69 ___-Cat

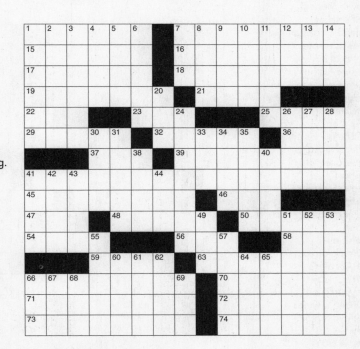

by Tibor Derencsenyi

48

ACROSS

1 Toast to one's health
6 Whooping ___
11 Belle of the ball
14 Humiliate
15 Ship from the Mideast
16 Commercial cousin of crazy eights
17 Traps off the coast of Maine
19 Get-up-and-go
20 Horn sound
21 Urns
22 Nozzle site
23 Southerner in the Civil War
25 "___ you asked . . ."
26 Part of a TV catchphrase from Howie Mandel
28 Ball catcher behind a catcher
31 Thesis defenses
32 Identical to
33 Twisted, as humor
34 Source of disruption to satellites
36 "My man!"
39 Disobeys
40 Letter-shaped skyscraper support
42 Sleeveless shirts
45 Strained relations?
46 Bakery fixtures
47 Goad
48 Moist, as morning grass
49 Los Angeles's San ___ Bay
52 Mayberry lad
55 Santa ___ winds
56 Gotham tabloid
58 Yank
59 Kennel club classification

60 Guy
61 Wide shoe spec
62 Put a hex on
63 Fish basket

DOWN

1 Pepper's partner
2 "Peek-___"
3 Jerry Lewis telethon time
4 Andrew Carnegie corp.
5 Investigator: Abbr.
6 Reef material
7 Steals, with "off"
8 Skin cream ingredient
9 New Jersey hoopsters
10 Places to see M.D.'s in a hurry
11 Company behind nylon and Teflon
12 Georges who composed "Romanian Rhapsodies"
13 "Little" shepherdess of children's verse
18 Daredevil Knievel
22 Serpentine sound
24 Droopy-eared hounds
25 Rink activity
26 This instant
27 Bobby ___, the only N.H.L.'er to win the Hart, Norris, Ross and Smythe trophies in the same year
28 Points on a diamond?
29 Roadies' loads
30 Corporate V.I.P.
32 Salon sound

35 Roswell sighting
36 Tall, skinny guy
37 Like vegetables in salads
38 Mantra syllables
39 Designer letters
41 Knee-slapping goof
42 Thus far
43 Street
44 Music genre for Enya
45 Aviation pioneer Sikorsky
47 Wash away, as soil
49 Andean land
50 Pitcher
51 Turns red, perhaps
53 "Survivor" setting, sometimes
54 And others, briefly
56 Peacock network
57 Col. Sanders's chain

by Randall J. Hartman

ACROSS

1 Language in which plurals are formed by adding -oj
10 Wrist timer
15 Christian Dior, e.g.
16 Drop a line from a pier, say
17 Angry rabbits in August?
19 Windsor's prov.
20 Prefix with identification
21 Hard-to-miss hoops shots
22 Handheld computer, briefly
24 Give a card hand
25 Hens at the greatest altitude?
32 Battery part
33 Houston skaters
34 Horse at the track
36 Villain's reception
37 Green card holder
38 Whence Goya's duchess
39 Memphis-to-Chicago dir.
40 Tourneys for all
41 Have ___ (revel)
42 Cat lady's mission?
45 Channel
46 Finder's ___
47 Shortly, after "in"
50 Have a bug
52 Tussaud's title: Abbr.
55 What a Chicago ballpark bench holds?
59 Apply, as coat of paint
60 Beach cookouts
61 Mensa-eligible
62 Private chat

DOWN

1 Greek nymph who pined away for Narcissus
2 "Any day now"
3 Any miniature golf shot
4 And more: Abbr.
5 Play about robots
6 Scents
7 Not yet final, in law
8 Trueheart of "Dick Tracy"
9 Poet's planet
10 Classifieds
11 Tree rings
12 Happy hour cry
13 Staff symbol
14 Dame Myra
18 Given experimentally
22 Many profs.
23 Actor Billy ___ Williams
24 Most calamitous
25 1944 Chemistry Nobelist Otto
26 Permanently written
27 "Take a look!"
28 Scouts seek it
29 Life form
30 China's Zhou ___
31 Luxurious fur
35 Guys' pals
37 Zeniths
38 French cleric
40 Luxuriant
41 Face on a fiver
43 Masthead title
44 On fire
47 Pointy tools
48 Impact sound
49 Informal "Welcome!"
50 Auto shaft
51 "___ first . . ."
52 Karaoke need
53 Track event
54 In ___ (existing)
56 Columbus Day mo.
57 Hoops org.
58 Rebellious Turner

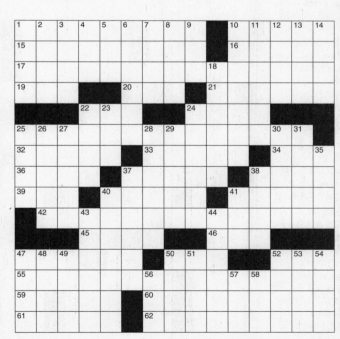

by Bruce Adams

50

ACROSS

1 "Vissi d'arte" opera
6 Rx, for short
11 Fed. holiday, often
14 Not just question
15 Evidence of pain
16 So-so grade
17 Part 1 of a snarky quote by 54-Across
19 D.C. clock setting
20 Admiral Bobby who directed the N.S.A. under Jimmy Carter
21 Unwordy
23 Prime status
24 Photo ___
27 Sibling of 54-Across
28 With 53-Across, noted comedy group, in brief
29 Geisel's pen name
32 ___-chef (kitchen #2)
33 "It's nobody ___ business"
35 Picks off, as a pass
37 Proposal fig.
38 Middle of the quote
41 Take steps
44 Showed fright
45 ___ Ark
49 "Cheers" character
51 Baseball exec Bud
53 See 28-Across
54 Speaker of the quote
56 General on Chinese menus
57 Celeb fired in 2007
58 Pale yellow Danish cheese
61 Ribbed, like corduroy
63 Japanese waist material?
64 End of the quote
68 Narrow inlet
69 Some are Dutch
70 Web mag
71 N.L. insignia
72 Iran-contra name
73 Prepare to fire again

DOWN

1 ___ Friday's
2 1st or 2nd, e.g.
3 Parties to a contract
4 Punch lines, e.g.
5 Menlo Park middle name
6 Farm enclosure
7 Golden parachute receiver, maybe: Abbr.
8 Actor Julia
9 Rombauer of cookery
10 Coll. course
11 Tennis star-turned-analyst
12 Antigone's father
13 What you pay
18 Slaughter in baseball
22 Western treaty grp.
23 Cockney's abode
25 Apothecary tool
26 Snowbirds' destination
30 Some OPEC officials
31 ___ Snorkel of the funnies
34 National Chicken Mo.
36 Thing to confess
39 Some batteries
40 Put into action
41 Firmly ties (to)
42 Share digs
43 Worth bubkes
46 Yerevan's land
47 Master escapologist
48 Radiator sound
50 Longtime Elton John label
52 Cap's partner
55 Bean on-screen
59 Record for later viewing
60 Anatomical canal
62 Golden ___ (senior)
65 "We know drama" channel
66 Sort of: Suffix
67 Pro ___ (for now)

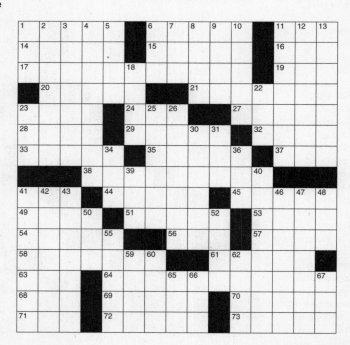

by Ed Early

ACROSS

1 Old ___ tale
6 Fiction's opposite
10 Two-wheeler
14 Novelist Zola
15 "Are you ___ out?"
16 Luau instruments, informally
17 Wee
18 Cost of an old phone call
19 Check for a landlord
20 Game equipment for an old sitcom star?
23 Son of Seth
24 Organic salt
25 Greek T
28 ___ Kippur
29 Chem. or biol.
30 Captains of industry
32 Sudden outpouring
34 Mark in "piñata"
35 Game location for an actress?
38 Major mix-up
40 Deflect, as comments
41 IBM/Apple product starting in the early '90s
44 Pull tab site
45 Pinup's leg
48 Product pitches
49 Carved, as an image
51 Florence's river
52 Game site for a popular singer?
54 Plastic building block
57 Mélange
58 When repeated, classic song with the lyric "Me gotta go"
59 Rainbow goddess
60 Pasta sauce first sold in 1937
61 Ponders
62 Like some Steve Martin humor
63 "___ It Romantic?"
64 "Give it ___!" ("Quit harping!")

DOWN

1 Actor Snipes of "Blade"
2 Prefix with suppressive
3 Owner of MTV and BET
4 New York Harbor's ___ Island
5 Order in a bear market
6 Faithfulness
7 Licoricelike flavor
8 Hand-to-hand fighting
9 8-Down ender
10 Singer Ives
11 "I Like ___" (old campaign slogan)
12 Barbie's doll partner
13 Inexact fig.
21 Train that makes all stops
22 Speaker's spot
25 Spilled the beans
26 &
27 "It's no ___!" (cry of despair)
29 Go all out
31 Like a mechanic's hands
32 Ump's call with outstretched arms
33 Paranormal ability
35 Tools with teeth
36 Wasn't turned inward
37 Tehran native
38 Place for a mud bath
39 Doze (off)
42 A ___ (kind of reasoning)
43 Maria of the Met
45 Bellyache
46 "___ Song" (John Denver #1 hit)
47 Not given to self-promotion
50 Winston Churchill flashed it
51 Love of one's life
52 Inquisitive
53 ___ mater
54 Gossipy Smith
55 Pitcher's stat.
56 Beefeater product

by Elizabeth A. Long

52

ACROSS

1 Chews the fat
5 Cleveland cagers, briefly
9 1986 Indy winner Bobby
14 ___ breve
15 Writer Waugh
16 Maine college town
17 Paper quantity
18 Zig or zag
19 Pooh's creator
20 *Line formatting option
23 Go off course
24 Blockbuster aisle
25 Prerequisite for sainthood
27 Nixon's 1968 running mate
30 Big top noise
31 Coke competitor
34 Not of the cloth
36 Pawn
39 In the style of
40 *Hipster
43 Cyndi Lauper's "___ Bop"
44 Accompanying
46 Explorer Zebulon
47 Book before Joel
49 Lacking slack
51 Get going
53 Kind of pool or medal
56 Common TV dinner
60 Part of Ascap: Abbr.
61 *Education overseers
64 Ring-tailed mammal
66 Jason's craft
67 Wharton degs.
68 Sought answers
69 Old female country teacher
70 Der ___ (Konrad Adenauer)
71 Model/volleyballer Gabrielle
72 Commoner
73 Coward of the stage

DOWN

1 Singer Brooks
2 Last Oldsmobile to be made
3 Britain's P.M. until 2007
4 Tennis star Pete
5 Grotto
6 Pub servings
7 27-Across, e.g., informally
8 "Get out!"
9 Cesar who played the Joker
10 "Exodus" hero
11 *College in Worcester, Mass.
12 One-year record
13 Lerner's musical partner
21 Sound reasoning
22 About, in dates
26 Satisfied sigh
28 "The Time Machine" race
29 Word following the last parts of the answers to the five starred clues
31 Pussy foot?
32 QB Manning
33 *Kids' game
35 "Ricochet" co-star
37 Rebel Guevara
38 Mauna ___
41 Fiber-___ cable
42 Pulsate
45 Prosciutto
48 Living room piece
50 Positive aspect
52 Self-assurance
53 Musician/wit Levant
54 Not tied down
55 Titleholder
57 Artist Picasso
58 Really steamed
59 Collectible Ford product
62 Voiced
63 Fairy-tale fiend
65 Private eye, slangily

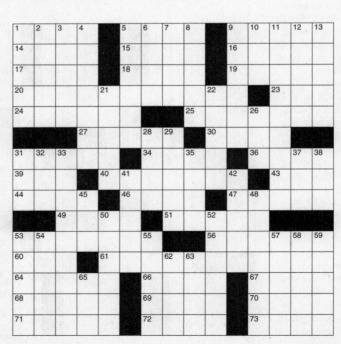

by Allan E. Parrish

ACROSS

1 Do very well (at)
6 Alabama march city
11 U.K. channel
14 Pope before Paul V, whose papacy lasted less than four weeks
15 Loud, as a stadium crowd
16 Yahoo! competitor
17 Result of hitting the pause button on a movie
19 Dundee denial
20 Have concern
21 Authoritative order
23 Vegetarian's protein source
26 Volcanic emission
28 The "B" in L.B.J.
29 Hall-of-Fame QB Johnny
31 Enzyme suffix
33 Low-lying area
34 Uncovers
35 Chief Pontiac's tribe
37 Coast Guard rank: Abbr.
38 Extra
40 Nightwear, briefly
43 Buses and trains
45 "Honest to goodness!"
47 Sit for a picture
49 ___ compos mentis
50 Try hard
51 Book size
53 NNE's opposite
55 Part of a list
56 Chatty birds
58 "The Censor" of ancient Rome
60 Tire pressure meas.
61 Old-time songwriters' locale
66 "Horrors!"
67 Online birthday greeting, e.g.
68 Go out
69 Go blonde, say
70 Seized vehicles, for short
71 Channel with cameras in the Capitol

DOWN

1 North Pole toymaker
2 Generation ___ (thirtysomething)
3 Cedar Rapids college
4 Carry out, as an assignment
5 Multitalented Minnelli
6 Bank fixtures
7 Goof up
8 Rich soil
9 "Goldilocks" character
10 Football bowl site
11 Dairy Queen offering
12 Overnight accommodations by the shore
13 John who starred in "A Fish Called Wanda"
18 Times on a timeline
22 Temperamental performer
23 TV, slangily, with "the"
24 ___ empty stomach
25 Attack before being attacked
27 Millinery accessories
30 "The Thin Man" canine
32 "Immediately," in the O.R.
35 ___ buco
36 Departed
39 Having been warned
41 Hepcat's talk
42 Appear to be
44 Derrière
46 Baltimore nine
47 Like some balloons, questions and corn
48 Playwright Sean
50 Ugly duckling, eventually
52 Person in a polling booth
54 A whole slew
57 Jacket fastener
59 After-bath powder
62 Con's opposite
63 Nascar unit
64 Longoria of "Desperate Housewives"
65 Desire

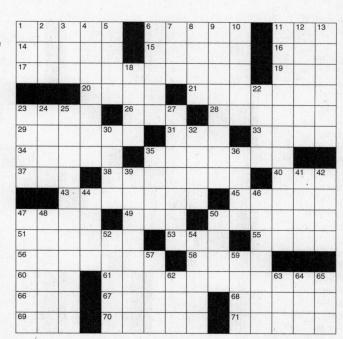

by Allan E. Parrish

ACROSS

1 Liquor holder in a coat pocket
6 Wonderment
9 Taxi sounds
14 Milk: Prefix
15 First word of every Robert Ludlum title but one
16 Extreme
17 Ward off
18 Texas tea
19 Sectors
20 "Just like that!"
22 Electronic toll-collecting system in the Northeast
23 Walk in water
24 In the past
25 "Not on your life!"
30 Torment
31 ___ in Show (Westminster prize)
32 Temporary drop
34 Subj. in drawing class
35 Cargo area
36 Rick's "Casablanca" love
37 Holiday ___
38 Planning detail
40 Gold standards
42 "Yeah, wanna start somethin'?"
45 War ender
46 Create, as a phrase
47 No-goodnik
50 "The Sopranos" clip? . . . or where you might hear 20-, 25- and 42-Across
54 Continent separator
55 Embargo
56 One of the Carpenters
57 Make joyous

58 Israeli-invented gun
59 Goaded, with "on"
60 Like notepaper or subjects of a king
61 Fed. monitor of stock fraud
62 Midterms and finals

DOWN

1 "Spare tire"
2 Content of some cones
3 Nailed
4 Farmer's headwear
5 Toiletries holders
6 Made amends (for)
7 Henry Clay, politically
8 Conger or moray

9 Army barber's specialty
10 Ran off to the marrying judge
11 Italian source of 2-Down
12 White House occupant: Abbr.
13 Snippiness
21 Midmonth time
22 Grandson of Adam
24 Love, honor and ___
25 Rear end
26 Heavens: Prefix
27 Taken ___ (surprised)
28 Religion with the Five Pillars
29 Small bite
30 "Bali ___"
33 Good time, slangily

35 Frequent target of engine wear
36 Circus animal enclosure
38 Tarnished
39 Walk to and fro
40 Old TV feature
41 Start of an Ella Fitzgerald standard
43 Timely news bulletin
44 Like some sacred art
47 Afrikaner
48 Legal rights org.
49 Successful conclusion of a negotiation
50 Labyrinth
51 Pieces of work?
52 Nair competitor
53 Conclusions
55 Vehicle with a route

by Daniel Kantor

ACROSS

1 Toyota Camry model
7 Dietary needs
11 Balaam's beast
14 1980 John Carpenter chiller
15 Sarcastic reply
16 Rap's Dr. ___
17 Channel swimmer Gertrude
18 Novelist Jaffe
19 Crude, e.g.
20 Back-to-the-slammer order?
23 Readies, briefly
24 "___ a traveler from an antique land": "Ozymandias"
25 Son of Judah
27 Opposite of ecto-
28 Hard-rock connector
29 Cheerful
30 Reason the kids were left alone?
34 Eiger, e.g.
37 A/C meas.
38 ___ Na Na
39 Get stuck with, as the cost
40 Reward for a Ringling invention?
44 In progress
45 La-la lead-in
46 Devil Ray or Blue Jay, for short
50 Prefix with cab or cure
51 Baba ___, Gilda Radner "S.N.L." character
53 Coward's lack
54 Scuff marks on the prairie?
57 Bespectacled dwarf
58 "Young Frankenstein" hunchback
59 TV's Howser
60 "Norma ___"
61 Poetic times
62 Museum guide
63 Since Jan. 1
64 Be in a stew
65 Alley pickups

DOWN

1 Grassy expanse
2 "Shoot!"
3 Looked like a wolf
4 Music from across the Atlantic
5 Diner basketful
6 Posthumous Pulitzer winner
7 Dalmatian's master, sometimes
8 Superior to
9 Group doctrine
10 Marquee topper
11 "Oklahoma!" gal
12 Ceylon, now
13 Condiment for pommes frites
21 Revolt
22 Go bad
26 Duma denial
28 Graphic ___
29 1970s tennis great Smith
31 Border on
32 Woman's shoe style
33 1969 and 2000 World Series venue
34 Put ___ on (limit)
35 1944 Hitchcock classic
36 Cranked out
41 Do
42 Least favorably
43 Starchy dessert
47 Hang around
48 Object of a tuneup
49 Turns to 0, say
51 It might be placed at a window
52 Without equal
53 Hawk's descent
55 Feudal estate
56 Throws in
57 Prohibitionist

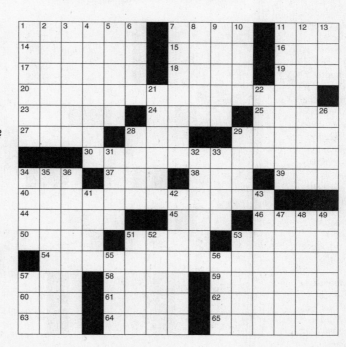

by Donna S. Levin

ACROSS

1 Morocco's capital
6 "Oh, my stars!"
10 Recipe amt.
14 They're not PC
15 Inner: Prefix
16 Pro ___ (one way to divide things)
17 African language family
18 Close
19 They can be refined
20 Ford explorer?
23 Jock: Abbr.
26 Sailor's affirmative
27 Mississippi city where Elvis was born
28 Hospital's ___ center
30 Positioned
32 Far Eastern bread
33 "The Hours" role for which Nicole Kidman won an Oscar
36 Genre for Aretha Franklin
37 Dashboard inits.
38 Pupil's locale
41 Billiards great
46 Org. with a complex code
48 ". . . ___ the whole thing!"
49 Rejoinder to "Am, too!"
50 With grace
52 Computer monitor: Abbr.
53 Bout enders, for short
54 Ambassadors and such, or an appropriate title for this puzzle
58 Ambience
59 Det. Tiger or N.Y. Yankee
60 Blow one's lid
64 Kind of mile: Abbr.

65 Cry out
66 Where the Decalogue was received
67 Shade trees
68 Talk back to
69 Ability

DOWN

1 Josh
2 Physician's org.
3 Roll-on brand
4 When Hamlet sees the ghost
5 Literally, "harbor wave"
6 One often seen in a turban
7 Fit for drafting
8 Ollie's partner
9 Friend of Hamlet
10 Jamboree group
11 Longtime Massachusetts congressman

12 Writer Shelby
13 Give, as a gene
21 Actress Cannon
22 Sport in which Israel won its first Olympic medal
23 Off-roaders, for short
24 ZZ Top, musically
25 Reckless
29 Trademarked fruit name
30 Discontinuance
31 Seuss's "Horton Hears ___"
34 "___ a man with seven wives"
35 Popular cereal or magazine
39 Langston Hughes poem
40 Discontinued fliers, quickly
42 River past Luxor
43 Rejects

44 Protective covering
45 Unaffected
46 Demented
47 Initiation, for one
51 French political divisions
52 Marine ___
55 Nolo contendere, e.g.
56 Unagi, in a sushi bar
57 Best-selling author Larson
61 Prefix with cycle
62 Chum
63 Up to, informally

by Kevan Choset

ACROSS

1 Exemplar of grace
5 Bidder's site
9 Fancy duds
14 Stay near the shore, say
15 1963 film "___ la Douce"
16 Eyeball benders
17 Pierce portrayer on TV
18 C
19 Raggedy Ann and friends
20 What a scary Doris Day did on the film set?
23 Cried a river
24 Congressional committee subject
27 Slippery sort
28 Nursery noise
30 Lather
31 More miffed
34 Talking birds
36 '60s muscle car
37 What the lexicographer/ dairy expert did?
40 Ring master?
41 Family nickname
42 Adam of "The O.C."
43 Air ball, e.g.
45 Math ordinal
46 RR depot
47 Sounded like a chick
49 Oracle site
52 What the paranoid C.I.A. publicist did?
56 Diet guru Jenny
58 Temple University team, with "the"
59 Snack with a lickable center
60 In reserve
61 River Kwai locale, formerly
62 Gem for some Libras
63 More together
64 Hill inhabitants
65 Auditioner's goal

DOWN

1 Give and take
2 Dylan Thomas's home
3 Build on
4 Weak brew
5 Tower designer
6 Hair twist
7 Gallic girlfriend
8 Prison exercise area
9 Beckett's no-show
10 Historical periods
11 Stern lecture
12 www bookmark
13 N.B.A. stats: Abbr.
21 Land south and west of the Pyrenees
22 Post-op program
25 Referred to
26 Bedtime request
28 See 29-Down
29 With 28-Down, noted 20th-century American artist, informally
31 Little rascal
32 Kukla's puppet pal
33 Scream and holler
34 Breath freshener
35 Understated
38 Bankrolls
39 Magician's secret exit
44 Repair, as film
46 Quakes
48 Fired up
49 C sharp equivalent
50 Comedic horn honker
51 Ultimate goal
53 Sluggin' Sammy
54 Victor's cry
55 Fish dish
56 Comedian Bill, for short
57 Some strands in a cell

by Richard Leva and Nancy Salomon

58

ACROSS

1 Jane Austen novel
5 Chopper blade
10 Friend
13 Meat cuts behind the ribs
15 Give the slip
16 Pharmaceutical giant ___ Lilly
17 Poker instruction
19 ___ v. Wade (1973 Supreme Court decision)
20 Elapsed time
21 Slowly merged (into)
23 Filling maker: Abbr.
24 Saudi export
25 "The final frontier"
27 Slots instruction
31 Burn with hot liquid
34 His and ___
35 Cousin of an ostrich
36 "Piece of cake!"
37 Diamond weight
39 Mojave-like
40 Mornings, for short
41 Boot bottom
42 Devoutness
43 Roulette instruction
47 Paris divider
48 Versatile truck, informally
49 ___ King Cole
52 Carafe size
54 Step-up
56 Critic ___ Louise Huxtable
57 Craps instruction
60 Chess pieces
61 Clear the blackboard
62 Breed of red cattle

63 Mammal that sleeps upside-down
64 Shut out
65 New Jersey five

DOWN

1 Castilian hero
2 Pitcher's place
3 Pitchers' gloves
4 Prelude to a deal
5 Carmaker's woe
6 Racetrack
7 Road goo
8 Strange
9 Closes again, as an envelope
10 Keep working hard
11 ___ vera
12 Told a whopper
14 Hide from view
18 Like Darth Vader
22 11-pointer in blackjack
25 Queens ball park
26 Sassy
27 Work at, as a trade
28 Pitched
29 Send forth
30 New York's Giuliani
31 The world has seven of them
32 Where soldiers stay overnight
33 Helper
37 Harry ___, Columbia Pictures co-founder
38 Sheltered, nautically
39 Be under the weather
41 How 007 does not like martinis
42 Squinted
44 Formerly known as
45 Orion, with "the"
46 Leave one's mark on
49 Unsophisticated
50 High-class tie
51 Parenting challenges
52 Ewe's baby
53 "I had no ___!"
54 Rick's love in "Casablanca"
55 Paradise lost
58 It's north of Calif.
59 Research room

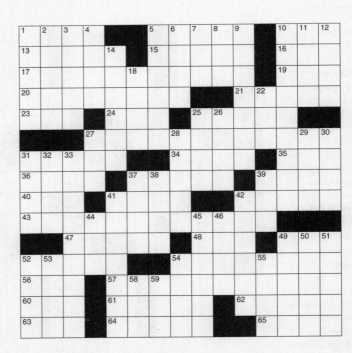

by Gordon Seaberg

ACROSS

1 The Beatles or the Stones
5 Penny
9 When repeated, a city in Washington
14 Inter ___
15 Penny, maybe, in poker
16 With 3-Down, French-born diarist
17 57-Across song about a request in a gene lab?
20 Not pro
21 Senescence
22 Prefix with dermal
25 Rocky hill
26 Prepare for printing
27 Prefix with gliding
29 Change over at a factory
31 Pulitzer or Tony, as for 57-Across
33 Star of Scorpio
37 57-Across song about a request in the maritime supply store?
40 Varnish ingredient
41 Dye chemical
43 Pouilly-___ (white wine)
46 Individual
47 Board game from India
51 Shade tree
53 Dover's state: Abbr.
54 Slothful
55 Word said twice before "Don't tell me!"
57 Noted Broadway composer

63 With 68-Across, what Fred MacMurray had in a 1960s sitcom
64 007
65 Famed lab assistant
66 Old catalog maker
67 Swear
68 See 63-Across

DOWN

1 ___-relief
2 Pint at a pub
3 See 16-Across
4 20th-century art movement
5 Synagogue singer
6 Whole
7 A degree
8 Golf bag item
9 Light switch surrounder
10 Battery end
11 Actress Turner and others
12 Lord or vassal
13 It's a plus in accounting
18 C.D. earnings: Abbr.
19 Howler
22 Mileage rating grp.
23 Manhandle
24 Pitcher Hideki ___
26 Honky-___
28 Give ___ for one's money
30 Heads' opposite
32 Small sharks
34 Followers of pis
35 Alleviated
36 Fence crossing
38 "Get it?"
39 53, in old Rome
42 Patriots' org.
44 Some patches
45 African antelopes
47 Fence features
48 ___ drop of a hat
49 Old Oldsmobile
50 Wishful one
52 Central
56 The one here
58 Brian Williams's employer
59 Old French coin
60 Bigheadedness
61 Charged particle
62 ___ Butterworth's

by Stephen Budiansky

ACROSS

1 Actress Thompson
5 Dye-yielding plant
9 Humble in position
14 Baseball great ___ Speaker
15 Paradoxical Greek
16 Far from 9-Across
17 Actors Holm and McKellen
18 Annual Broadway event
20 Travolta musical
22 Woolly, e.g.
23 Met debutante of 1956
26 Talking computer of film
29 Bikini, for one
30 War stat.
31 Coin rating
32 Aware of
34 Baffin Islander
36 Theme of this puzzle
40 Dunk, e.g.
41 Sp. miss
42 "The Time Machine" people
43 Mattress problem
44 "Vive ___!"
49 Pick up
50 Football's Gang Green
53 Play too broadly
55 Online newsgroup system
56 Predatory players
60 Follower of H.S.
61 Crop up
62 Trusses
63 Shuttle protector
64 Like Waldorf salad apples
65 Goofball
66 Cheap digs: Abbr.

DOWN

1 Scarlet letter, e.g.
2 Genesis landfall
3 Moolah
4 Tear into
5 Cortez's victim
6 Start of some movement names
7 "Vacancy" shower
8 New Orleans campus
9 Defeater of Holyfield, 1999, for the world heavyweight title
10 Pearl Buck heroine
11 Terrier type
12 India inc.?
13 "Indeed"
19 Moira's player in "On the Beach"
21 Respectful greeting
24 Mine, in Marseille
25 Tennis's Davenport
27 ___ brat
28 Bossy but generous type, supposedly
31 "Suspicion" studio
33 Wash. setting
34 Erhard movement
35 Menaces, in a way
36 Corduroy rib
37 Understood by few
38 Hit the trails
39 So
40 Pray
43 Having had a good workout
45 Spits out
46 Painter of bathers
47 Verdi opus
48 Yucca fibers
50 Beat (out)
51 Ordinal ending
52 ___-Finnish War
54 Gds.
56 Dirty dog
57 "Exodus" hero
58 "Road" film destination
59 G, e.g., but not H

by Alan Arbesfeld

ACROSS

1 Lavish entertainment
5 At a distance
9 Russian country house
14 Realtor's unit
15 Exploration org.
16 Actor Hawke
17 Title for Jesus
20 Chi-town team
21 Slimmer's regimen
22 Contents of Bartlett's
23 Peddle
24 Mows
25 Lightest-colored
28 Pre-dye hair shade, often
29 Revolutionary Guevara
32 Champion tennis servers
33 Russia's ___ Mountains
34 "Slow down!"
35 1976 Walter Matthau/Tatum O'Neal movie
38 Private investigators, for short
39 Iranian money
40 Africa's Sierra ___
41 Suffix with book or freak
42 Baseball glove
43 Expired
44 Smooth, as a drive
45 One of the three H's in a summer weather forecast
46 Gas rating number
49 Coarse fiber
50 "Ugh!"
53 1958 best seller by William J. Lederer and Eugene Burdick
56 Concise
57 Shakespeare's stream
58 Major-___ (bigwig)
59 Name on a deed
60 Store
61 One more time

DOWN

1 Chief parts of adipose tissue
2 Sound in a long hallway
3 Big-mouthed carnivorous dinosaur, for short
4 Hosp. brain readout
5 Make sacred
6 No longer bright
7 Aide: Abbr.
8 The old college cheer
9 Second-in-command
10 One of the Three Musketeers
11 Atkins of country music
12 Big-eared hopper
13 "No ifs, ___ or buts"
18 Texas oil city
19 Is, in math
23 Predicate parts
24 Words moving along the bottom of a TV screen
25 Singer Page
26 Suffers after overexercise
27 Bloodsucker
28 Terrific
29 Total confusion
30 Singer Lena or Marilyn
31 Relaxed
33 Come together
34 Tearful
36 Twaddle
37 Sports jacket
42 Christmas display sight
43 Underlying
44 Temporary halt
45 Comedy
46 Director Preminger
47 Prepare to swallow
48 Beach bird
49 Coffee, slangily
50 Universally known figure
51 Arrived
52 "Well, what do you ___?!"
54 Thanksgiving side dish
55 Boise's home: Abbr.

by Janet R. Bender

62

ACROSS

1 Sign at an A.T.M.
5 Smooth
11 Afternoon social
14 Slender instrument
15 Without delay
16 Columnist Buchwald
17 Actress Moore
18 Ringers
20 Freshwater fish with silvery scales
22 For each
23 Cone producer
25 Punch hard
28 Tiny bit
29 Ringers
33 Actress Hatcher
34 Vessel of 1492
35 Ringers
42 Calais concept
43 Ones with war stories
45 Ringers
51 Tater
52 Butcher's, baker's or candlestick maker's
53 Western tribe member
54 Equips with metal plating
57 Indispensable
59 Ringers
62 Hit the spot
65 Air hero
66 In abundance
67 Some investments, for short
68 Noted Turner
69 Aft ends
70 Certain cobras

DOWN

1 Cape ____
2 Justice Fortas
3 Shade maker for a siesta
4 ____ to the throne
5 Deli meat
6 Kind of clock or number
7 Additionally
8 Voter's finger stainer
9 Scholastic sports grp.
10 Cry of pain
11 Assume responsibility for
12 Raises
13 Confused
19 Late afternoon on a sundial
21 Educated guess: Abbr.
23 Hale
24 Checked a license, informally
26 Trigonometric function
27 Director Kazan
30 Quick drink
31 Old cable TV inits.
32 Jokester
36 Indy 500 locale
37 Summer N.Y. hrs.
38 Hula hoops?
39 A Gabor
40 Habitués
41 Manuscript annotation
44 Copenhagen-to-Prague dir.
45 Evergreen
46 All excited
47 Favorite
48 Rule
49 Showy blooms
50 Encountered
51 Nasser's successor
55 Semis
56 Ella Fitzgerald specialty
58 Largest of seven
60 Barley brew
61 Craggy prominence
63 Utilize
64 Double-180 maneuver

by Gene Newman

ACROSS

1 Fraternity letter
4 Battery contents
8 Oldtime actress Todd
14 Personal
15 Goof off
16 Attack
17 Stop on it
18 No neatnik
19 Anxiety
20 Cartier's Christmas creation?
23 In any way
24 Stat for Sammy Sosa
25 Thimblerig thing
27 Meal
30 Ones soon to leave the ivied halls: Abbr.
31 Subcompact
32 American Revolutionary portraitist
34 Illegal act, in slang
35 Capote's least favorite road sign?
39 Olympus competitor
40 "I'm in!"
41 Just
42 "Noble" element
43 Woven fabrics
48 Narc's employer: Abbr.
49 Fall from grace
50 12 chimes
51 Songbird's lament?
57 Sounded like a Persian
58 Point to the right
59 Driver's org.
60 Shed
61 Shade of green
62 Comic strip cry
63 Didn't go straight
64 Scored the same
65 Like few counties nowadays

DOWN

1 Drink at the Duke's Head
2 Deviate
3 Completely committed
4 Likewise
5 Massage target for a runner
6 Popular shirt maker
7 Actress Mazar
8 All ___
9 City on the Hong River
10 Tied
11 Absolute
12 "Le Cid" composer
13 Got the fare down
21 Chapter of history
22 Collar
26 Run on TV
28 Hand measure
29 Hué New Year
30 Swings around
31 Wild West
33 Big name in fashion
34 Montana Indian
35 Johnny Unitas wore it
36 Norman's home
37 Diminutive, as a dog
38 Rug rat
39 Silent agreement
42 Prepared for action
44 Gerund maker
45 Lit
46 More protracted
47 Sly
49 Computer honcho Wozniak
52 Jedi ally
53 Play Shylock
54 Hideaway
55 Man, but not woman
56 Be hot and bothered
57 Miss after marriage

by Richard Silvestri

ACROSS

1 French cleric
5 Enthusiasm
9 Slightly open
13 "Time ___," 1990s sci-fi TV series
14 1950s candidate Stevenson
16 Art ___
17 56-Across figure
19 Bushy do
20 Birds' homes
21 Stabbed
23 Job application attachments
24 "Bird on ___," 1990 Mel Gibson movie
25 Carrier to Sweden
26 Before: Abbr.
27 Necessary: Abbr.
30 ___ Parks, former "Miss America" host
33 Two under par
34 Man's nickname that's an alphabetic run
35 W.C., in England
36 56-Across figure
38 Metal in rocks
39 Popular card game
40 When some TV news comes on
41 Change for a five
42 Superman's symbol
43 Brings into play
44 Singer Sumac
46 Faux pas
48 Fierce one
52 Vance of "I Love Lucy"
54 Place to buy a yacht
55 Mimicked
56 S. Dakota monument

58 ___ of Man
59 Happening
60 Johnson who said "Ver-r-r-y interesting!"
61 Loads
62 Puts in extra
63 Spick and span

DOWN

1 Battling
2 Indian who may be 1-Down
3 Foundation
4 Tire out
5 Cutups
6 A sphere lacks them
7 Computer keys: Abbr.
8 Neighbor of a Vietnamese

9 Firefighter Red
10 56-Across figure
11 Farm unit
12 Crucifix
15 Place to dip an old pen
18 "___ la Douce," 1963 film
22 Actor David of "Separate Tables"
24 Laser gas
26 Walks outside the delivery room?
28 To be, in France
29 Opposite of an ans.
30 Ocean-colored
31 Millions of years
32 56-Across figure
33 Set foot in
36 Mrs. Bush

37 "My treat!"
41 One who rows, rows, rows the boat
44 Breadmakers' needs
45 Algebra or trig
47 Walt Disney World attractions
48 Headed (for)
49 Taking out the trash, for one
50 Heart line
51 Chirp
52 Colorado resort
53 ___ facto
54 Partner of born
57 Dam project: Abbr.

by Sherry O. Blackard

65

ACROSS

1 Retreats
7 Dry, as wine
10 It leaves marks on asphalt
14 Triumphant cry
15 Word often said twice before "again"
16 Numbers game
17 She wed George Washington
20 Niagara Falls' prov.
21 Karel Čapek play
22 Church nooks
23 Where Washington relaxed
28 Wrath
29 Pi preceder
34 Friend in the Southwest
37 Forsaken
39 Ready for picking
40 State defense organization headed by Washington
43 Its flight attendants' greeting is "Shalom"
44 Magician's start
45 Word prefixed with poly-
46 Edison's New Jersey lab locale
48 "Welcome" site
49 Where Washington's forces wintered
55 Defense aid
59 Writer Fleming
60 Time Warner merger partner
61 Colonial force headed by Washington
66 ___ Stanley Gardner
67 Belfry flier
68 ___ corpus
69 Faculty head
70 Not just tear up
71 "Tristram Shandy" author

DOWN

1 Televised sign in football stands
2 Hersey's bell town
3 Love of artistic objects
4 D.C. summer clock setting
5 Fed. biomedical research agcy.
6 Deprive of food
7 Fab Four drummer
8 Directional suffix
9 Dancer Charisse
10 Old record problem
11 Popular sneakers
12 "Picnic" playwright
13 Female deer
18 ___ date
19 Rajah's wife
24 Carp
25 "Star Trek: T.N.G." counselor
26 Bellini opera
27 Prefix with potent
30 "The Count of Monte ___"
31 Film director Martin
32 Mayberry boy
33 Close
34 Swear to
35 Actor O'Shea
36 Investments usually held for yrs. and yrs.
37 Kind of suit found in a courtroom
38 Sculling need
41 Queen in "The Lion King"
42 Page (through)
47 Chapter 57
48 Avian talkers
50 Needing a good brushing, say
51 Ingest
52 Scarcer
53 Beatnik's encouragement
54 "Family Ties" mom
55 Served past
56 Oral tradition
57 "To Live and Die ___"
58 Bingo call
62 Peacock network
63 Musical talent
64 Long.'s opposite
65 Face on a fiver

by Ed Early

66

ACROSS

1 Chest adornment
6 Candidate for rehab
10 Somewhat, in music
14 Really go for
15 Boffo review
16 Apricot-shaped
17 Valentine's Day pastries?
19 Make rhapsodic
20 Top of a suit?
21 Mrs. Chaplin
22 Hardly suited for Mensa
23 Director Craven
24 Rainy months?
27 Sword handles
29 Pickled delicacies
30 A lot of binary code
32 Asian nurse
33 ___ mater (brain covering)
36 Subtly added mistakes? . . . or a title for this puzzle
41 Part of marbling
42 Wild revelry
43 Rainfall measure
44 Suffix with buck
45 Areas usually decorated with stained glass
48 Attempt to score in hockey?
52 New Deal inits.
55 Viking attire
56 Teen spots?
57 Sibling, e.g.: Abbr.
58 "Yikes!"
59 Fork in a mountain pass?
62 Zola heroine
63 ". . . ___ sum"
64 Try to bite
65 They lack refinement
66 It's held at eateries
67 "Later, dude!"

DOWN

1 Colorful parrot
2 Draw forth
3 Horse player's buy
4 "Exodus" hero
5 Went first
6 Father of the Titans
7 Port south of Osaka
8 Time to revel, perhaps
9 Hi-___ graphics
10 Pretend to be
11 Pizza places
12 Playground retort
13 Bygone
18 Stallion, once
22 Indian metropolis
25 2004 Boston conventioneers, informally
26 One of a Navy elite
28 Sun Devils' sch.
30 Clocked out
31 Anti-Brady Bill org.
32 In the least
33 Line of suits?
34 "Monsters, ___" (2001 animated film)
35 Bone china component
37 Column style
38 Will or fist preceder
39 Really eager
40 Pizza
44 Nike rival
45 Blessing evoker
46 Swimming site
47 Suds holders
48 Minutes taker, maybe
49 Indiana senator Richard
50 Really dumb
51 Needing a lift
53 5/8/45
54 Prince Valiant's lady
59 Hesitation sound
60 Public radio host Glass
61 Compete

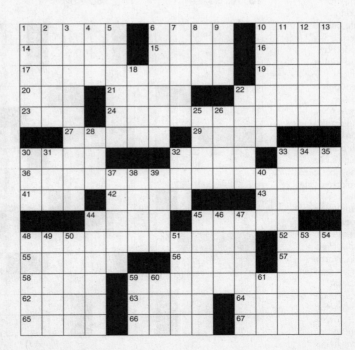

by Lee Glickstein

ACROSS

1 Livens (up)
5 Snapshot
10 Bedazzles
14 Away from the wind
15 Home run slugger Hank
16 Retail store
17 Glib responses
19 On the ocean
20 Baffled
21 Canines or bicuspids
23 New Haven collegians
24 Personal bugbear
27 Observer
30 Quattros, e.g.
31 Some sports cars
34 Take into custody
37 Supreme Diana
38 Go bad
39 Indy service break
41 Sport ___ (all-purpose vehicle)
42 Med. school subj.
44 Caviar source
45 Price add-on
46 Subway handhold
48 Make into law
50 Kind of stove
53 Smooch
56 Major company in metallic products
57 Drink often served with a lemon twist
60 Skin woe
62 Portfolio hedges
64 Eliot or Frost
65 One of the nine Muses
66 "Lohengrin" soprano
67 Drags
68 Heroic tales
69 Not shallow

DOWN

1 Mama's partner
2 Fill with joy
3 Flower feature
4 Protect, as freshness
5 Free ticket
6 Hems' partners
7 Source of iron or lead
8 Rich pastry
9 Beginning
10 Not an expert
11 Exhausted
12 Before, in verse
13 Depot: Abbr.
18 "Forget it!"
22 Clean air org.
24 "Blue Hawaii" star
25 Far-reaching view
26 "The Private Lives of Elizabeth and ___" (1939 film)
28 Common newspaper nickname
29 Art Deco designer
31 Understand
32 Jay Silverheels role
33 Go back to square one
35 Surprise greatly
36 Roman robe
40 Bundle
43 Things held by Moses
47 Chest muscle, for short
49 Neatened
51 Easy strides
52 Designer Ashley
54 Item worn around the shoulders
55 Pick up on
57 Teensy bit
58 Navy noncoms, for short
59 "Rush!" order
60 It may be a walk-up: Abbr.
61 Dove's sound
63 Children's game

by Marjorie Berg

68

ACROSS

1 Film mogul Louis B. (whose company mascot was 26-Across)
6 "Funny!"
10 Hard to fluster
14 Mrs. David O. Selznick, daughter of 1-Across
15 Assist in wrongdoing
16 Hodgepodge
17 One lacking courage
19 On the briny
20 ___ Tuesday
21 Take the first step
23 Poland's Walesa
25 Tam sporter
26 Roarer in film intros
29 Sty fare
31 Eucalyptus-loving "bears"
35 Drive-thru dispenser, maybe
36 Gazetteer statistic
38 Sporty Mazda
39 Courage seeker in a 1939 film
43 Top man in the choir?
44 ___ proprietor
45 SSW's opposite
46 Fake
48 Crowe's "A Beautiful Mind" role
50 Suffix with chariot
51 Pack and send
53 Reply to "That so?"
55 Deuterium and tritium, to hydrogen
59 Make unreadable, for security
63 Island near Java
64 One feigning courage
66 Tied in score
67 "___ homo"
68 Put ___ in one's ear
69 An earth sci.
70 Not fake
71 Cake sections

DOWN

1 Fail to catch
2 Keystone's place
3 Reunion number
4 Sign up
5 Superman player George
6 Barn loft contents
7 Basics
8 Puts on the burner
9 Tear into
10 Formal jacket feature
11 What's more
12 In ___ of
13 A drawbridge may span one
18 Render harmless, perhaps, to 26-Across's kin
22 Hardly cramped
24 Round dances
26 Starbucks order
27 Old anesthetic
28 Prophetic signs
30 Argentina's Juan
32 Frankie or Cleo
33 Do penance
34 Less dotty
37 Ike's two-time opponent
40 Exerting little effort
41 Straight: Prefix
42 Former Georgia governor Maddox
47 Sleeping bag closer
49 Suggest subtly
52 Treaty result
54 "Star Wars" genre
55 "___ to differ"
56 Except for
57 Promise product
58 Shelter org.
60 Gape at
61 Whitetail, e.g.
62 Notable times
65 Slithery swimmer

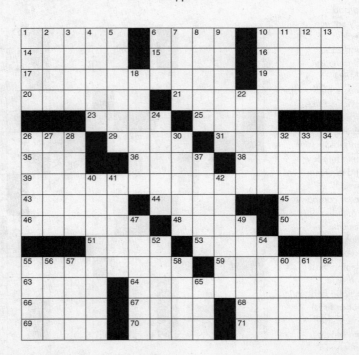

by Gilbert H. Ludwig

ACROSS

1 Strip ___
5 Favored by God
10 Wielding a peeler, maybe
14 Locket shape
15 Instant message sender, perhaps
16 Disney lioness
17 Purse item
18 Popular group dance
20 Like dessert wines
22 Top-2% group
23 "Ich bin ___ Berliner"
24 Travelers' org.
26 Plod along
28 Toasters do it
34 River islet
35 Farmer's letters?
36 Salinger title girl
40 Desk set item
44 Van ___, Calif.
45 Enter again
46 Neighbor of Braz.
47 Four-runner?
51 Break into parts, as a monopoly
54 Hoo-ha
55 "Big Blue"
56 Unwelcome forecast
60 Potter's potions professor
64 One with a half-interest
67 Laundry item
68 Earthen pot
69 Commercial prefix with liner
70 Grant for a film?
71 Lone Star State sch.

72 Rodeo critter
73 Girl or boy lead-in

DOWN

1 Comfy footwear
2 Swear to
3 ___ duck
4 Lands' End competitor
5 Dickensian epithet
6 Warp-and-weft machine
7 Actress Sommer
8 Glimpsed
9 Soap opera meetings
10 A Beatle bride
11 In one's natural state
12 Movie set light: Var.

13 John of "Miracle on 34th Street"
19 Peel
21 1970's Japanese P.M. ___ Fukuda
25 Not "fer"
27 Worked with
28 ___ Crunch
29 Place
30 Humble response to praise
31 Pick up
32 Felt under the weather
33 Taints
37 Most of it nowadays is filtered
38 ___ mortals
39 Many an M.I.T. grad: Abbr.
41 U.S.A.F. rank

42 "Nana" author
43 Old oath
48 Sign of disuse
49 Self-assurance
50 Friend on "Friends"
51 Exquisite trinket
52 Letter-shaped fastener
53 Prepare to get shot?
57 Water holder
58 Course on insects, for short
59 Fork-tailed flier
61 "I smell ___"
62 Left side
63 "Only Time" singer
65 Quick rest
66 Bird in the "Arabian Nights"

by James M. Jenista and Dana McLemore

ACROSS

1 Look at, as stars
5 Artist's suffix with land or sea
10 Tortoiselike
14 "___ Around" (#1 Beach Boys hit)
15 Breaking a bad one is good
16 El ___, Tex.
17 ___-a-brac
18 Big kitchen appliance maker
19 Eight, in Spain
20 Wife of King David
22 Prepare to pop the question
23 Nova Scotia clock setting: Abbr.
24 June 14
26 Hamburger meat
30 Peter who is an eight-time Oscar nominee
32 Last full month of summer
34 Departure's opposite: Abbr.
35 Penny
39 Cheater's aid
40 Yellowish shade
42 Asian nurse
43 President before Wilson
44 Australian hopper, for short
45 Igloo dweller
47 "To be or not to be" soliloquist
50 Woman of "Troy"
51 One taking flight
54 That, in Tijuana
56 Scent
57 "Days of Our Lives," for one
63 "The World According to ___"
64 Ne plus ___

65 Slightly
66 Feminine suffix
67 Full . . . and happy about it
68 Mideast's ___ Strip
69 Active one
70 Cursed
71 School before middle school: Abbr.

DOWN

1 Any of the Bee Gees
2 Taj Mahal site
3 Time, in Mannheim
4 Work on glass, say
5 Former Iranian leaders
6 Awoke
7 Basic rhyme scheme
8 "H.M.S. ___"
9 Third letter after delta
10 Light dessert
11 Donned skates, e.g., with "up"
12 Actor Milo
13 Sheeplike
21 Declares
22 ___ Kan (pet food)
25 Peter who played Mr. Moto
26 Agreement
27 Atmosphere
28 End-of-week cry
29 Noisy public speaker
31 California/ Nevada lake
33 Singer nicknamed the Velvet Fog

36 Oscar winner Jannings
37 Partner of rank and serial number
38 Ending with tele-
41 Side dish at KFC
46 "Scram!"
48 Old Turkish title
49 Ripper
51 Ran amok
52 Poetry Muse
53 Talent
55 Ditchdigger's tool
58 Director Preminger
59 Newspaper unit
60 And others, in footnotes
61 Completely demolish
62 One who raised Cain
64 Inits. in Navy ship names

by Christina Houlihan Kelly

ACROSS

1. Actor Damon
5. Great buy, slangily
10. Go yachting
14. Met solo
15. Inventor Nikola
16. Ides of March utterance
17. Timid creature
18. Big name in chips
19. "Hud" Oscar winner
20. Actor Ben with the gang?
23. ___-mo
25. Cornhusker State: Abbr.
26. Like good soil
27. Chops to bits
29. Best Actress winner for "Million Dollar Baby"
31. Really enjoyed
32. Democratic honcho Howard
33. Roadside sign
36. Marathoner Frank with candy?
40. Layer?
41. Richly adorn
42. Easy mark
43. Nutty as a fruitcake
45. Motor City hoopster
46. Mel Ott, notably
48. Several eras
49. Unlock, poetically
50. Novelist Evan with a small smooch?
54. Man Friday, e.g.
55. Publicist's concern
56. Workbook segment
59. Puts into play
60. "Our Gang" dog
61. Mower maker
62. Document content
63. Dorm annoyance
64. Cashless deal

DOWN

1. "Spy vs. Spy" magazine
2. "You ___ here"
3. Gets soused
4. Pucker-producing
5. Metro entrances
6. Potato sack wt., maybe
7. Renaissance family name
8. K.C. Royal, e.g.
9. Space cadet's place
10. Author/illustrator Maurice
11. First-stringers
12. Europe's "boot"
13. Quiet time
21. Like a stumblebum
22. ___ compos mentis
23. Not just a success
24. Like a ballerina
28. Despicable sort
29. Serta competitor
30. Harry Potter accessory
32. Icicle former
33. Become familiar with
34. Fabulous author
35. "Funny Girl" composer Jule
37. Voyages in vain?
38. Place for a title
39. Used to be
43. Up-to-the-minute
44. White Monopoly bill
45. "I yam what I yam" speaker
46. False front
47. Encyclopedia volume
48. Landscaper's tool
50. ___ monde
51. "You said it!"
52. Defense grp.
53. Roster removals
57. Lyrical Gershwin
58. Blouse, e.g.

by Deb Amlen

ACROSS

1 Light ___
6 Defender of some unpopular causes, in brief
10 "Jabberwocky" starter
14 Father ___ Sarducci of "S.N.L."
15 Game delayer
16 "I can't ___ thing!"
17 Comedy troupe since the '60s
20 Org. with bomb-sniffing dogs
21 Gull-like predator
22 Enter cautiously
23 The Joads, e.g.
25 Features of some cell phones
26 Breakfast bowlful
28 "Really?!"
29 Milk: Prefix
30 Gives a rap
31 Hogwarts letter carrier
34 Bellicose god
35 Propelled a shell
36 Peau de ___ (soft cloth)
37 Part of w.p.m.
38 Orbital point
39 ___ nova
40 Slips on a slip
42 Housekeeper, at times
43 Lights into
45 Margaret Mead study site
46 From there
47 Geeky sort
48 Nashville sch.
51 Momentous

54 Double contraction
55 Egyptian Christian
56 Bubbling over
57 Poetic adverb
58 Gas brand in Canada
59 Like unwashed rugs

DOWN

1 Fuji competitor
2 Exec
3 Military part-timers
4 Chemical suffix
5 "William Tell" composer
6 Giant slain by Hermes
7 Water-to-wine site

8 Beyond tipsy
9 Cold
10 Prickly plant
11 London rail hub
12 Places in the heart
13 Composer Camille Saint-___
18 Swedish chain
19 Chair designer Charles
24 Hobby shop stock
25 Nuclei
26 Brouhaha
27 Bern's river
28 MTV teen toon
30 Broadway rosters
32 Cheeky
33 Shakespearean king
35 Shimmer

36 Passable
38 "If I Were ___ Man"
39 Short end of the stick
41 Blusterer
42 1960s–70s Dodge
43 Had home cooking
44 Parasol's offering
45 Brief tussle
47 Drops off
49 Piqued state
50 Beyond homely
52 Sounds from Santa
53 Baseball card stat.

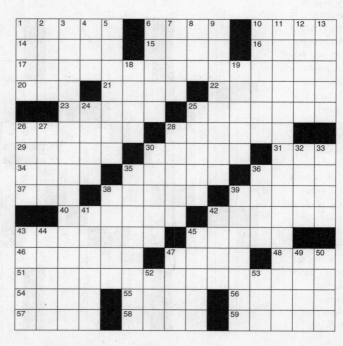

by Rob Richardson

ACROSS

1 Baldwin of the silver screen
5 Recur, as arthritis
10 Father of Seth
14 Actress Hatcher
15 Computer item with a tracking ball
16 Aura being picked up
17 Possibly prompting a reply like 25-, 47- or 62-Across
20 Supersede
21 Immature insects
22 Rink surface
23 Rep.'s opponent
24 Singer Sumac
25 "What?!"
31 Companion of Tarzan
32 It's good only for its waste value
33 T-bone or porterhouse
37 Not so much
39 Noted Tombstone family, once
41 Ancient Roman censor
42 Like beer at a bar
44 River's mouth
46 Sign outside a hit show
47 "What?!"
50 Railroad stop: Abbr.
53 End of a proof
54 Chem. thread
55 Meat-packing pioneer
57 Chosen one
62 "What?!"
64 Slugger Sammy
65 Sailor's "Halt!"
66 "The Thin Man" wife
67 European car
68 Nigeria's largest city
69 Son of Seth

DOWN

1 "___ additional cost!"
2 Pope after Benedict IV
3 Folies Bergère designer
4 Kind of acid
5 Atmosphere, as in a restaurant
6 For both sexes
7 Toothpaste holder
8 "It's no ___!"
9 Shotgun shot
10 State unequivocally
11 Split (up)
12 At right angles to a ship
13 Jason's ally and lover, in myth
18 Killer whales
19 Poetic feet
23 Horse with a spotted coat
25 Sign of a saint
26 Unlock
27 Toward sunset
28 Swapped
29 Sheik's bevy
30 And others: Abbr.
34 Facility
35 Gillette brand
36 Wacko
38 Problem with an old sofa
40 Hollywood hopefuls
43 Resentment
45 "Li'l ___" (Al Capp strip)
48 Springlike
49 "Phèdre" playwright
50 Final approval
51 Custer cluster
52 Entertain
56 Kind of history
57 For men only
58 Studebaker's fill-up, maybe
59 Daffy Duck or Porky Pig
60 Continental currency
61 Those: Sp.
63 Eggs

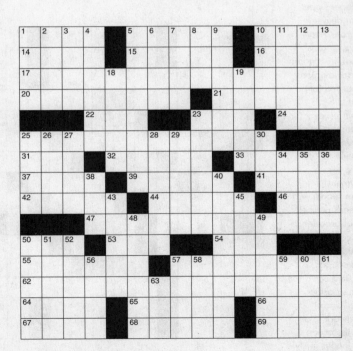

by Robert Malinow

ACROSS

1 Frisks, with "down"
5 Muhammad's birthplace
10 Elisabeth of "Leaving Las Vegas"
14 Ranch unit
15 Pong maker
16 Hoopster Malone
17 "All I Wanna Do" singer, 1994
19 Toledo's lake
20 Pekoe server
21 Luggage attachment
23 Threw in
24 French article
26 Like woolen underwear?
27 Salsa scooper-uppers
29 Sun. delivery
30 Yeats or Keats
33 Boys' or girls' room, in London
34 Attack by plane
37 Cleansed (of)
38 First U.S. chief justice
40 Hide-hair link
41 No longer in style
43 Press for payment
44 Palm reader, e.g.
45 Hither's partner
46 Rigid bracelet
48 Bill of fare
50 Needle hole
51 Gut course
55 All riled up
57 Rich's partner
58 Say "Uncle!"
59 "Network" star
62 On the ocean
63 No longer in style
64 Add kick to
65 Flat rate?
66 Late actor Davis
67 Chapters of history

DOWN

1 Orzo, e.g.
2 Had a yen
3 Radial pattern
4 Eve's tempter
5 Fountain offering
6 Catchall abbr.
7 Cougar or Lynx
8 Hags
9 Sony competitor
10 Summer pest, informally
11 "The Bridge" poet
12 Dickens's ___ Heep
13 Mournful poem
18 Luke Skywalker's mentor
22 Like the air around Niagara Falls
24 "Looks like trouble!"
25 Lunchtime, for many
28 Congealment
30 Country club figure
31 Mideast export
32 Singer with the 1988 #1 country hit "I'm Gonna Get You"
34 Acted the fink
35 Antagonist
36 Flub
38 Leigh of "Psycho"
39 Month for many Geminis
42 Difficult spot
44 Mariner's measure
46 Guardian Angels toppers
47 Table extension
48 New dad's handout
49 Biscotti flavoring
52 Salvage ship's equipment
53 New Mexico's state flower
54 Cookout leftovers?
56 ___ facto
57 For the asking
60 Profs' helpers
61 Yalie

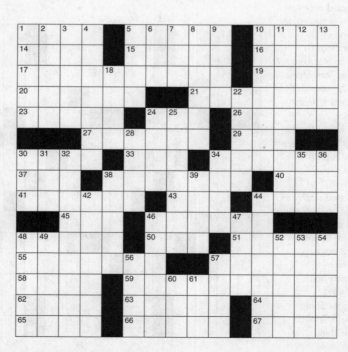

by Gail Grabowski

ACROSS
1 Service unit
7 Itinerary abbr.
10 Blunders
14 Garner of jazz
15 "Get it?"
16 Nair competitor
17 Watergate judge John
18 Biblical jawbone source
19 Way off
20 "No kidding!?"
23 Give, as odds
25 Untrustworthy sort
26 Up ___ (trapped)
27 Really attractive
32 Tolkien creature
33 Stop by
34 Hugs, in a letter
35 Drugs, briefly
36 Trip to the Bahamas, e.g.
40 "Doonesbury" character based on Hunter S. Thompson
43 Rock's Bon Jovi
44 Pushed hard
48 Genetic material
49 "The Mothers-in-Law" co-star
52 Bone: Prefix
54 Bend shape
55 European carrier
56 Jimmy Carter autobiography
61 Zilch
62 Narrow inlet
63 Habituates
66 Blue-pencil
67 Creature with a tiny waist
68 Bar request
69 "___ Dinah" (Frankie Avalon's first hit)
70 Range units: Abbr.
71 Word spelled phonetically by the starts of 1-, 20-, 27-, 36-, 49- and 56-Across

DOWN
1 French possessive
2 "___ tu" (Verdi aria)
3 In formation
4 Rope fiber
5 Develop sores
6 Dabble in
7 Biblical twin
8 Hardy heroine
9 Ricky player in '50s TV
10 Put on the books
11 Grid coin tosser
12 Collide with, in a way
13 D and C, in D.C.
21 Like Nasdaq trades
22 Xanthippe, e.g.
23 Peggy with the 1958 hit "Fever"
24 Novelist Rand
28 Job for Perry Mason
29 Chanteuse Lena
30 Marker
31 "There's ___ in 'team'"
35 Old World blackbird
37 1977 double-platinum Steely Dan album
38 Playing hard to get
39 More morose
40 Blotted (out)
41 Expose to the sun
42 Grasshopper's cousin
45 Stomach-related
46 Stat. for Pedro Martínez
47 Letters on a shingle
49 "Kitchy-___!"
50 Waggle dance performer
51 Victoria's prince
53 Related maternally
57 Vehicle on rails
58 Glasses option
59 Boaters and bowlers
60 Muslim mystic
64 Yellowstone herd member
65 Like some grins

by Holden Baker

The New York Times

CROSSWORDS

SMART PUZZLES PRESENTED WITH STYLE

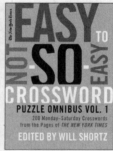

Available at your local bookstore or online at nytimes.com/nytstore.

1

```
J U L E P   V A I N   M A S S
A L E V E   E L M O   I L L S
M A N E T   R O H E   X O U T
  N I N E T Y S I X H O U R S
    S R I   S P I E L
I T S O P E N   T H O M A S
P A H   A R O A R   G A S P
O C E A N S T W E N T Y T W O
D E B T   A L L A H   T A R
S T A N Z A   O N E C E N T
    O S S I E   C A Y
F A N T A S T I C E I G H T
E L O I   I A G O   S N I P E
T E E M   S L E D   L E E K S
A X L E   T Y R A   E T S E Q
```

2

```
T I E S   U N P C   G I J O E
A D Z E   N E R O   O S O L E
L O R D   D U O S   E M A I L
C L A U D E R A I N S   N O S
    C D R O M   O M A R
H A B E A S   U N A L I K E
I D I   Y E A H S   D A V I S
R E L S   A T 2 A M   S E T S
A L L O R   N O F E E   R E A
M A Y B E S O   G L A S S Y
  O S H A   A G A I N
A M C   E T H E L W A T E R S
S I E N A   A R E A   L U A U
O N A I R   F I A T   E R I E
F I N E D   T E N T   R O D S
```

3

```
A P S O   O S C A R   R I N K
G A U L   F L A R E   E D E N
A U D I   F O R E S T F I R E
S L A V   O R A T E   O V A
P I N E S A P   A C T E D
    B U D S   L O S E
A N D R E A   D E R E L I C T
R O N A   G R E E N   E C O N
P R A N C E R S   A B R U P T
    C A S S   S T A Y
S H A H S   P E A S O U P
C O B   T O T A L   T U N E
A V O C A D O P I T   A T T N
L E V I   D I S C O   L I I I
P L E A   S L E E P   K E E N
```

4

```
L I S P   G R A C I E   I L E
A S I A   R E R U N S   D O E
R I T A   A L A R M C L O C K
I N C R E D I B L E H U L K
A T O   L E T   E X A L T
T O M E I   U S E R   T E A
  T S H I R T S   A R T S
  G R E A T G A T S B Y
R A R E   T H E B E A R
A B O   D E E D   B A B E L
P R O M O   A C R   I N E
  A M A Z I N G K R E S K I N
T H E R I V I E R A   C I G S
O A R   N O T N O W   O N M E
P M S   G R E E N S   T I A S
```

5

```
S C A M P   B O G S   R A N D
U L N A E   O R N E   A R O O
B A C H E L O R P A R T I E S
S M E A R S     N E E D L E
    Y E A R   A P E D
  M A S T E R B E D R O O M
A L A N S   G A I N S   T R A
G A G A   E L T O N   D E E R
E L I   R E A C T   C O R O T
D O C T O R Z H I V A G O
    O B I E   C E R F
C O M E O N   N E I G H S
A M A T T E R O F D E G R E E
P I T A   S O F A   R H E A S
S T A G   S T A N   S T Y L E
```

6

```
R O V E R   M O M S   F A Z E
E N E R O   A L A I   A R I D
B A R R T E N D E D   R I N G
A N Y   A M O S   E N R A G E
      S T I R   W A I F
C A S T O R   C A R N E G I E
A L T A R   T R I M   T E M P
B A E R   T H A T S   C A S E
O M A R   R E F S   T H R E E
T O M S W I F T   C H E S T S
      H A F T   C O E D
A Y E A Y E   B O M B   S H E
H A R P   C A R R P O O L E D
E L I E   T R I G   S N A R E
M E N D   A C T I   S E V E N
```

7

```
A R A B I C   M S G   A M A S
N I N E T Y   A P E   R I L L
S C A R E D Y C A T   E D I E
E C C E   E O N   B A D G E
L I T T L E A N G E L   A N T
      O T S   L E E R Y
D E F E N D   R E L E A S E R
E V I T E   F E D   D R U I D
N E S T L E R S   S I E N N A
      H E I N E   L I N
O C T   E V E N I N G S T A R
C H A I R   T E M   M U L E
C O I N   G R A P E J E L L Y
U R L S   P I T   S A L L I E
R E S T   A P O   A L L E N S
```

8

```
D I D S O   B A T H   F T D
O M I T S   E R R E D   R O O
P A R I S H H O U S E   E R N
A C E R   O E D S   L A S S O
      F A R M   S E T S H O T
I N P R I S O N   L A S H
L L O Y D   T E S S   T E N D
E E L   A S H H E A P   R O E
T R I S   A S I T   A M B L E
      S H U N   S U N V I S O R
S C H O L A R   P O E T
I N H O T   A S S N   C Z A R
T O A   R O S H H A S H A N A
A T M   A R T O O   M U Z A K
R E S   Y A W P   A M U S E
```

9

```
D E C O   C A P O   G L O W
E N O L A   H O O K   R E D O
I N D E X C A R D S   A M O K
S U E   E R S T   A Z U R E
M I D D L E M A N A G E R S
      E S E   O T I S
S L A M   I O W A N   U F O
P U T O N E S F I N G E R O N
A X E   A L L A N   K N E E
      E R L E   E V E
   P I N K Y T U S C A D E R O
C E D E S   L I O N   D E G
U S E R   R I N G L E A D E R
S T A G   I R A N   S P I K E
P O L Y   M E S S   T E S S
```

10

```
B O O R S   H U M   U N J A M
U B O A T   I S O   N E A T O
D I Z Z Y D E A N   E X X O N
G E E Z E R   T O A T
E S S   U T T E R S   F W D
      F U Z Z Y Z O E L L E R
H A S A M E A L   A O N E
O M E N S   R E M   C U R D S
P A I N   N O O N D A Y S
O Z Z Y O S B O U R N E
N E E   C H A L E T   S S S
      K E E N   I D O T O O
M A G N A   J A Z Z Y J E F F
I N P E N   O V A   E A T A T
G N A W S   S E P   S I S S Y
```

11

```
E D W A R D  ■  Q T R  ■  H A S P
Q U A K E R  ■  W Y O  ■  I T A L
U L T I M A T E P U R P O S E
A L T O  ■  W I R E T A P P E D
L Y S  ■  C E N T  ■  E G O  ■ ■
■ ■  F O R  ■  Y A M  ■  S K I P
A U D E N  ■ ■  K H A N  ■  I S R
U S I N G O N E S N O O D L E
L S D  ■  O N B Y  ■  V J D A Y
D R O P  ■  T A B  ■  S A S  ■ ■
■ ■  A V A  ■  O L E S  ■  H B O
E X A C E R B A T E  ■  H E A P
Z O N I N G O R D I N A N C E
R U I N  ■  E N D  ■  N I M R O D
A T N O  ■  T D S  ■  G A M I N S
```

12

```
A P E S  ■  P A R C H  ■  S K I S
M O M A  ■  A L C O A  ■  K I N K
R U B B E R B A N D  ■  A N T I
A R R I V E  ■  S I S  ■  N E D
D I A N E  ■  S O U T H B E N D
I N C  ■  R A H A L  ■  E R A S E
O G E E  ■  Y U K  ■  F E A R E D
■ ■  S P E L L B I N D  ■ ■
P A S T A S  ■  A L F  ■  Y M C A
A L I E N  ■  S W E E P  ■  C O G
J A M E S B O N D  ■  L U C R E
A M P  ■  Y A W  ■  M A R L O N
M E S A  ■  G E R M A N B U N D
A D O S  ■  E T H A N  ■  A R E A
S A N K  ■  L O O P Y  ■  N E T S
```

13

```
Z E S T S  ■  G R A B S  ■  G E E
A F T R A  ■  L A R U E  ■  O L D
G R O U C H O M A R X  ■  L I E
S E W N  ■  O R E  ■  B U R D E N
■ ■  M E D D L I N G  ■  A R F
■ ■  L E D A  ■  A L L R I S E
A M I E S  ■  S S E  ■  E T S
B E N D I N G T H E R U L E S
A N A  ■  O O P  ■  E N D T O
B U T T S I N  ■  S W A B  ■ ■
■ ■  R A H  ■  G H O U L I S H
T E A B A G  ■  Y R S  ■  A L A R
H A N  ■  R E V E R S E S I D E
O T C  ■  I N A N E  ■  D E C A F
U S E  ■  F E R A L  ■  O D E T S
```

14

```
T R I O  ■  S C A B  ■  A T E A M
I O N A  ■  M A G I  ■  D R A M A
M O T H  ■  I N R E  ■  H E R O N
■ ■  F O U N T A I N P E N N Y  ■ ■
■ ■ ■  O E D  ■  N E R D  ■ ■ ■
B U R R O  ■  A F I R E  ■  C B S
A S I A N S  ■  L A I  ■  H A I L
B A S K E T B A L L F A N N Y
A G E E  ■  A A R  ■  S I L A G E
R E N  ■  O G L E D  ■  C O L O R
■ ■  O N E L  ■  O O H  ■ ■
■ ■  H O T C R O S S B U N N Y  ■ ■
P A S T A  ■  O K I E  ■  E A V E
E T H E L  ■  N U N S  ■  A P E X
P E A R L  ■  S A G E  ■  T E S T
```

15

```
W A L K  ■  P A W N  ■  S A M B A
I L I E  ■  A C H E  ■  U L E E S
R A C E  ■  P R I X  ■  B I Z E T
E M I L I O E S T E V E Z  ■ ■
D O T  ■  L O S T  ■  M E N A C E
■ ■  A S S  ■  S I R  ■  N A M
E X T R A E F F O R T  ■  I R A
A H E M  ■  E C O  ■  A N T I
T O L  ■  E L E C T R I C E E L
U S E  ■  D I D  ■  E T E  ■ ■
P A M P A S  ■  G A P E  ■  P A Y
■ ■  E A S T E R N E M P I R E
A S T I N  ■  B A J A  ■  A Q U A
L O R N E  ■  R I O T  ■  T U B S
F L Y E R  ■  O N U S  ■  H E A T
```

16

```
A M I E   C H O P S   H O W L
M A L L   H A N O I   A R I A
F U L L T I M E S T U D E N T
M I S S A L   S H U N   O D E
      C D I   E P I C
N E W Y O R K E R   T O T I E
O C H O   E E L   E R R O R
S L E W   N A I L S   N I N O
E A R L E     Z O O   E N I D
S T E E L   H A L F P R I C E
      D I C E   A T E
O T T   T A R A   S T A N Z A
P H A S E S O F T H E M O O N
A R C H   I N T R O   M I N D
L U T E   O S S I E   O R E S
```

17

```
R O I L   F A B L E   T S A R
O R C A   O B O E S   U P T O
O N E W H O C A N T   B E A M
F O R M A T   S E P   E R A
      A I R   R E E L E D I N
C H A N G E H I S M I N D
A I L   S A P   N O E L S
S E L E C T S   A B Y S M A L
E D D I E   A P E   O N O
    A N D W O N T C H A N G E
B I Y E A R L Y   L E M
I L L   R I D   O R A T E S
B I O S   T H E S U B J E C T
L A N K   H A T E D   O T O E
E D G Y   E T O N S   R E N T
```

18

```
I M A C S   L A G   S C A L A
M O R A L   O V A   C O D E S
S P I N A L T A P   R U R A L
      D Y E S   B E G O N E
A B B Y   V A N N A W H I T E
F L A B B Y   B I N   S T O P
A U R A L   L A N A I
R E D R O S E   O L D S A L T
      C H E S S   E A G E R
A D E S   O Z S   S A Y I D O
B A N K B R A N C H   O N A N
A T T I R E   A E O N
C I R C A   H O L D W A T E R
U V E A S   A L L   E R A S E
S E E P S   Y E S   D A R T S
```

19

```
P E T E   S M I T   E F R E M
A V I A   M A T A   M A O R I
N O B R A I N E R   S T A I N
S K I N F L I N T S   T R E X
Y E A   R E F   S I T U
      M O S E S   N I E C E S
P I O U S   S T R E S S O U T
A M C S   S T Y E S   D O R A
C A T C H C O L D   S A L O N
S C A L A R   E A R L Y
      E D U C   L E E   A L E
A C D C   B O N E H E A D E D
S A R A N   S C R A P I R O N
S P A R E   T A T S   L E N A
N O T S O   S A S H   S P A S
```

20

```
P I S A   A T B A T   A T A D
I D E S   C O R P S   R A B E
T I C K L E P I N K   I C U S
T E T E A T E T E   L A H T I
      D Y A D   A M I N O
A R T I S T   T I N M A N
L I O N   E X X O N   A E R O
L A E     O X X     T E N
O T T S   B O X O F   R E N E
T A H I T I   L E E R A T
    E R I C A   B A W L
H I L L S   S T A G E A C T S
O H I O   C H I L D S P L A Y
J O N I   S E L M A   S A L S
O P E N   A N T S Y   E M I T
```

21

A	L	A	N	■	T	A	D	A	■	E	S	T	E	S
S	A	N	E	■	O	L	E	S	■	Q	U	A	K	E
H	U	G	O	B	L	A	C	K	■	U	M	B	E	R
E	R	R	■	I	D	S	■	T	E	A	M	U	S	A
N	A	Y	S	A	Y	■	M	O	N	T	E	■	■	■
■	■	P	L	A	Z	A	■	D	E	R	I	V	E	■
A	S	S	A	Y	■	E	R	L	E	■	S	M	E	W
M	O	W	N	■	L	A	K	E	R	■	T	U	N	A
A	L	A	I	■	A	L	E	G	■	R	O	S	I	N
J	E	T	S	K	I	■	T	O	P	I	C	■	■	■
■	■	■	H	A	N	K	S	■	E	D	K	O	C	H
S	E	T	F	R	E	E	■	S	A	G	■	C	H	A
E	X	I	L	E	■	M	I	N	C	E	M	E	A	T
M	E	L	E	E	■	P	O	O	H	■	C	A	L	E
I	S	L	A	M	■	T	C	B	Y	■	I	N	K	S

22

H	A	R	K	■	A	W	A	S	H	■	K	E	L	P
A	S	E	A	■	R	O	T	T	E	N	I	D	E	A
D	E	E	R	A	F	E	M	A	L	E	D	E	E	R
E	A	S	E	L	S	■	■	L	E	N	D	L	■	■
S	T	E	E	L	■	B	R	I	N	E	■	W	E	E
■	■	■	M	I	C	R	O	N	■	■	T	E	A	L
A	P	P	■	S	A	A	B	■	I	G	N	I	T	E
D	R	O	P	O	F	G	O	L	D	E	N	S	U	N
M	O	L	I	N	E	■	C	U	E	R	■	S	P	A
I	N	I	T	■	D	O	R	E	M	I	■	■	■	■
T	E	C	■	T	R	I	P	E	■	A	N	I	O	N
■	■	E	T	H	O	S	■	■	O	N	E	T	W	O
N	A	M	E	I	C	A	L	L	M	Y	S	E	L	F
F	L	A	T	S	C	R	E	E	N	■	S	M	E	E
L	I	N	E	■	O	M	A	N	I	■	E	S	T	E

23

B	A	S	T	E	■	S	W	A	B	■	A	B	E	D
A	T	E	U	P	■	H	A	L	O	■	S	A	S	E
N	O	D	E	S	■	A	D	E	N	■	C	R	A	W
A	M	A	■	I	T	R	I	E	D	T	O	B	U	Y
N	I	K	O	L	A	I	■	A	R	T	■	■	■	■
A	C	A	M	O	U	F	L	A	G	E	S	U	I	T
■	■	A	N	T	■	A	M	E	X	■	T	O	E	■
F	E	A	R	■	S	P	Y	■	C	E	N	T	■	■
O	A	F	■	S	H	O	E	■	G	S	A	■	■	■
B	U	T	I	C	O	U	L	D	N	T	F	I	N	D
■	■	S	A	L	■	C	A	R	E	F	O	R	■	■
O	N	E	A	N	Y	W	H	E	R	E	■	T	M	I
S	E	R	A	■	C	O	I	L	■	T	E	H	E	E
L	A	I	C	■	O	R	E	L	■	C	L	E	A	R
O	R	E	S	■	W	E	D	S	■	H	I	N	T	S

24

S	K	I	M	P	■	I	L	L	S	■	F	E	E	D
C	A	R	O	L	■	B	E	A	U	■	A	X	L	E
A	N	I	M	A	L	M	A	G	N	E	T	I	S	M
R	E	S	■	C	A	S	K	■	L	A	T	T	E	S
■	■	■	H	A	M	■	■	R	I	T	E	■	■	■
V	E	G	E	T	A	B	L	E	G	A	R	D	E	N
E	C	O	L	E	■	E	I	G	H	T	■	A	X	E
N	O	R	M	■	D	A	V	I	T	■	F	L	A	W
O	L	E	■	G	E	T	E	M	■	R	E	A	C	T
M	I	N	E	R	A	L	D	E	P	O	S	I	T	S
■	■	■	M	A	D	E	■	■	L	S	T	■	■	■
S	A	L	I	N	E	■	B	L	U	E	■	B	O	Y
T	W	E	N	T	Y	Q	U	E	S	T	I	O	N	S
A	O	N	E	■	E	U	R	O	■	T	R	A	C	E
G	L	O	M	■	S	I	G	N	■	A	S	T	E	R

25

L	A	S	S	O	■	D	A	D	S	■	H	O	T
Y	A	L	T	A	■	M	U	S	I	C	■	O	L	A
C	H	A	R	T	T	O	P	P	E	R	■	P	I	N
R	E	B	A	■	A	D	E	S	■	I	T	S	O	K
A	D	S	P	A	C	E	■	E	P	I	C	■	■
■	■	■	B	E	L	L	B	O	T	T	O	M	S
S	A	C	H	E	T	■	E	R	N	■	H	T	M	L
O	B	O	E	S	■	B	A	R	■	M	E	C	C	A
A	L	D	A	■	S	E	R	■	M	I	S	H	I	T
K	E	E	P	A	N	E	Y	E	O	N	■	■	■
■	■	N	E	L	L	■	M	U	D	B	A	T	H
P	R	A	D	O	■	I	M	I	T	■	A	L	V	A
R	I	M	■	N	O	N	E	T	H	E	L	E	S	S
I	C	E	■	Z	O	O	M	S	■	B	E	R	E	T
X	E	S	■	O	H	N	O	■	W	R	O	T	E

26

```
WHEW  ECOL  OSKAR
ROAR  NORA  PUNNY
YETI  DREW  EMOTE
   TURNONANAXIS
ITSTRUE   BET
TUNEINTOMORROW
NSYNC   REM  ABED
OKD  HEYBABY  LIE
WEEP  POI   ALIGN
 DROPOUTOFSIGHT
   PAC   TOILETS
  TIMOTHYLEARY
OLIVE  MILL  PEWS
SIREN  COLE  AVIS
HEART   ANOD  DAZE
```

27

```
MARCH  TMAN  ARMS
GLARE  AUTO  COAL
ROTOROOTER   CLUE
STEPONIT   TILDE
    SITS  HANDSET
TOR  NOT  AFTER
ADOBE   NRA  NOUN
LIMO  RANDR  TYPE
KEPT  ISE   ASCOT
  ETATS  OWL  ENS
ACROBAT   RASP
HARMS   PANORAMA
EROS  ROUNDROBIN
ALOU  RUNG  ATEST
DAMP  SITE  NOLTE
```

28

```
ROC  SNARL  TENAM
CLU  PIXIE  UVULA
CDE  ACEOFSPADES
OPTSTO  TEA  EXT
LAIC   JSBACH
ALPHAMALE   OUST
   ERITU  WASTES
LEADEROFTHEPACK
AROUSE  FIORI
WALL   DENMOTHER
  EMBODY   AONE
AKA  ORG  MILTIE
MARLBOROMAN  KGB
ENLAI  UTILE  EMO
STOOL  NODOZ  YAK
```

29

```
ATAD  SPAT  ATTAR
LAME  TORO  NAURU
IDOL  ALAN  GORED
TAKINGABYTE  NAY
    VEER  ALAS
WIPERS  REPORTS
HOARD  DIVE  MYTH
INC  SLIVERS  LEE
PIKE  AMEN  OPERA
 COASTER  NURSED
  FRAT   PISA
ILL  NEVERSAYDYE
RAYED  AXIS  IRON
ARENA  LIMA  NAUT
NASAL  ETON  GYRO
```

30

```
SUBS  SLID  STAMP
OGRE  TERI  NEPAL
FLATBROKE  EMOTE
TISSUE  STRAPPED
   STEM   ODE
NCAA  TAPAS  RAVE
AUDIO  RADIO  NIT
FEELINGTHEPINCH
TIP  LOOIE  EVIAN
ANTS  STORM  EERO
   PHI   EACH
INTHERED  PEARLS
HOSER  TAPPEDOUT
OPART  CREE  IOTA
PEREZ  HERD  TMEN
```

31

```
P E R E Z ■ D Y E R ■ F I S T
A L A M O ■ E A V E ■ I N C H
S L I P O F T H E T O N G U E
T A N ■ ■ E E O ■ V I O L S ■
■ W I N D S O R C A S T L E ■
K E E N E S T ■ O A T ■ S S S
G R A T E ■ J O N E S ■ ■ ■
B A R R ■ K N O T S ■ I C O N
■ ■ O W L E T ■ A T O N E ■
A S P ■ O E R ■ U N W A X E D
S Q U A R E D A N C E R S ■
K U R T S ■ T S O ■ ■ W E E
F I S H E R M A N S W H A R F
O R E O ■ D O R A ■ H O I S T
R E D S ■ S N I P ■ A G N E S
```

32

```
G T O S ■ U R S A ■ A B H O R
A O U T ■ R O A M ■ T R O V E
G O T O P L A N B ■ P A T E S
A T O L L ■ D E U C E ■ D R E
■ F E A S T ■ S R A ■ O D A
D U G ■ T H E C H I C A G O L
O N A L E A S H ■ P E W ■
S O S A ■ T I C ■ O S A Y
■ K E V ■ L O I S L A N E
S L E E V E L E S S T ■ L O S
T I N ■ I R A ■ T R E S S ■
E E C ■ L A N C E ■ N E A T O
A L O N E ■ D E L I O R D E R
M O R E Y ■ I L L S ■ T I M E
S W E D E ■ S T O P ■ A P P S
```

33

```
A D A M S ■ H A M S ■ M R E D
R E N E W ■ O M A N ■ Y O Y O
M A N N A ■ F A T E ■ B O R N
■ L A D Y O F T H E L A K E
■ ■ B R A ■ Z E D ■
M A C R A E ■ D I E D ■ P G A
E T H I C ■ S O F A ■ N O R M
C H I C K E N O F T H E S E A
C O M E ■ T O N Y ■ E A S E S
A S P ■ H O W E ■ C A T E R S
■ E M U ■ B E D ■
■ G E M O F T H E O C E A N
N O R A ■ F O A L ■ A R I E S
A N T I ■ E A R L ■ S O L V E
P E E L ■ E D D Y ■ E S S E X
```

34

```
A T O Z ■ R E H A B S ■ E W E
D A V E ■ E D E N I C ■ X E R
I C E S ■ G A M E K E E P E R
N O R T H A M P T O N M A ■
■ ■ S O L E ■ E A R E D
A R E ■ W E S T P O I N T N Y
L A P S E ■ R A W ■ A N T E
O T I C ■ J O Y C E ■ T E R P
N I C O ■ I D O ■ A E R E O
S O U T H B E N D I N ■ S E T
O N R I O ■ ■ E N D S ■
■ E A S T L A N S I N G M I
P L A N E T A R I A ■ A E O N
A Y N ■ R O T T E N ■ F L U X
Y E S ■ S P H E R E ■ U S E S
```

35

```
(T)H E ■ J A I ■ I M P A C (T)
O I L W E L L ■ A R E A M A P
Y E S I S E E ■ M A N L E S S
■ N S C ■ (T)S Q U A R E
P A I G E ■ (T)O(T) ■ S C I
A N N E ■ (T)E N E(T) ■ E N D E
L A N D(T)A X ■ L O(T) ■ D I A
A C E(T)I C ■ P A T I O S
D I R ■ (T)I S ■ N O T M A N Y
E N C E ■ (T)A R O(T) ■ O N N O
■ I V E ■ (T)U(T) ■ E B S E N
C R O S S A(T) ■ E L I
L O C K S I N ■ B U E L L E R
A L L E A R S ■ A L G E B R A
(T)I E D Y E ■ D A Y ■ O A(T)
```

36

```
S C A T   A D A M S   A C H E
H A R E   R E B U T   S H O T
I R O N   E L E N A   P A T S
P A S S F A I L C L A S S
S T E E R     H E S   E S S
      S E P I A     S W A T H
A G A   Y E S N O A N S W E R
T U T U   T A T A R   W A V E
O N O F F S W I T C H   Y E W
M I N O R     C H O I R
S T E   A L E     R O L E S
    T R U E F A L S E T E S T
C L I O   A L L A H   A P S O
H A M S   F A T S O   T E E N
E Y E S   S T A T E   E R N E
```

37

```
E L I A   A B B E     D R A W
M A R C   T R A C T   E A C H
I M A C   P E T R I   S P R Y
T E Q U I L A S U N R I S E
      R N A       G A G
R E D S K Y A T M O R N I N G
A R I E S   G E O D E   T O R
T A M   B O N U S     A T E
E T A   B A R O N   F A L S E
D O G D A Y A F T E R N O O N
    A L A     A A A
  A F T E R T H E S U N S E T
A X I S   E R A S E   I O W A
M E N U   A U R A L   A H E M
A D E N   E M U S   S O R E
```

38

```
B O E R   A S S T D A   P T A
A R C O   H O O R A H   O O P
S A L A M A N D E R S   I T T
S C A R A B   O S E   O N A N
E L I E L   D I S M A N T L E
T E R R A C E     E L I T E S
S S S   Y E A H   G O O D S
      M I D D L E M A N
S T R A D   S P A M   T A S
T H E M E S     R E S C A L E
P E R M A N E N T   P O R T A
A S E A   A L A   B U N T E D
U P A   K I L I M A N J A R O
L O D   O L I V I A   O R E G
S T S   A S S E S S   B E D S
```

39

```
C A R A T S   C H E   C R A B
O N E C U P   H A L   L A N A
S T U C C O W A L L   A M E N
A S P   S T I F F A R M I N G
      F O S S E   O U S T S
J A S O N     C O O P
A L I E   S P E E D S   G U Y
W O R S E C O N D I T I O N S
S T E   G O T T E N   R I D E
      C A T S     D O N O R
S W O R D   A S P E N
T I M E S T A B L E S   F A A
E L I A   B E F O R E H A N D
A C T S   A R A   E R M I N E
D O S E   R O B   S T O R E S
```

40

```
T A B O O   G A M E   B A I T
A L L A H   I B A R   O N C E
O P A H S   J E S T   S T I R
  C U T T O T H E Q U I C K
E L K   O D E     U N C L E
S I T U P S   G A L A   S E L
P A I R     P R O O F S
  R E L I G I O U S F A S T
    S N A P A T   L I O N
I M P   E D E N   T I E D O N
N A A C P     P O D   E N E
J O N A T H A N S W I F T
O R E S   A R I A   D A R T S
K I L T   W E N T   I R I S H
E S S E   N A E S   T E P E E
```

41

C	H	O	P		F	O	N	Z		C	E	L	S	
L	I	N	A		U	L	E	E	S		U	F	O	S
O	A	S	T		R	A	T	A	T	A	T	A	T	T	A	T
S	T	E	R	O	L		L	O	V	E				
E	A	T	I	N		S	M	O	K	E		L	O	U
S	L	S		E	S	T	A	T	E	S		E	O	N
			G	U	L	A	G				E	N	Z	O
	H	A	P	P	Y	B	I	R	T	H	D	A	Y	
S	E	M	S			C	A	S	E	S				
O	L	E		O	N	D	A	T	E	S		F	E	W
C	L	X		K	O	O	L	S		S	T	A	R	E
		S	E	C	S			S	O	B	E	R	S	
D	I	R	T	Y	H	A	R	R	Y		I	R	A	S
E	V	E	L		E	G	G	O	N		R	O	T	O
N	E	M	O		E	S	O	S		D	E	A	N	

42

M	A	M	M	A	L		Y	E	S	M	A	A	M
E	R	I	T	R	E	A		A	R	R	E	A	R	S
S	E	A	S	T	A	R		C	A	T	N	A	P	S
			I	O	N	S		H	O	A	D			
A	L	A	N	I	S		A	T	F		E	T	C	
C	O	L	A	S		P	B	S		D	R	O	O	P
C	O	L	I		A	I	D		C	O	S	E	L	L
E	N	E		O	C	T	O	P	U	S		R	O	E
N	I	G	G	L	E		M	O	P		T	I	N	A
T	E	R	R	A		J	E	D		S	I	N	E	S
	S	O	O		T	I	N		S	I	N	G	L	E
		W	O	R	N		T	H	E	Y				
R	O	A	D	T	A	X		B	A	R	T	A	B	S
P	R	A	I	R	I	E		A	R	R	I	E	R	E
M	A	R	M	O	T	S		I	A	M	S	A	M

43

T	O	T	A	L		E	L	L		I	D	A	H	O
A	E	R	I	E		F	E	E		G	I	V	E	R
B	R	I	D	G	E	F	I	N	A	N	C	I	N	G
	P	A	S	T	E		S	L	I	T				
P	O	L		C	T	R		I	T	A	S	C	A	
O	V	E	R	T	H	E	E	D	G	E		T	O	D
D	A	C	H	A		N	A	H		E	R	A	S	
	T	R	O	U	B	L	E	D	T	I	M	E	S	
B	I	O	S		R	A	W		D	I	E	T	S	
R	O	W		W	A	T	E	R	F	I	L	T	E	R
A	N	N	I	E	S		D	O	A		L	D	S	
		N	T	S	B		G	I	N	Z	A			
S	O	N	G	B	Y	P	A	U	L	S	I	M	O	N
K	O	A	L	A		O	W	E		E	M	P	T	Y
A	F	T	E	R		E	L	S		C	A	S	T	E

44

O	R	C	A	S		R	A	P		W	E	A	V	E
N	E	A	T	O		I	K	E		O	L	L	I	E
E	L	B	O	W		V	I	N	E	R	I	P	E	N
T	A	B	L	E	T	E	N	N	I	S				
W	I	E	L	D	E	R		R	E	A	D	E	R	
O	D	D		T	R	I	K	E		G	I	V	E	
			D	R	A	N	O		Q	U	A	I	L	
	A	R	E	N	A	F	O	O	T	B	A	L	L	
P	R	A	D	A		T	I	L	E	S				
O	C	T	A		A	S	L	A	N		D	I	E	
T	H	E	M	O	B		I	T	S	S	A	F	E	
			F	I	E	L	D	H	O	C	K	E	Y	
B	U	B	B	L	E	G	U	M		P	R	O	V	O
O	H	A	R	A		A	L	A		H	A	T	E	R
P	S	H	A	W		D	U	N		S	P	A	R	E

45

O	L	D	S		C	O	M	A		C	O	O	L	S
R	I	O	T		U	S	E	D		A	L	C	O	A
S	A	G	E	B	R	U	S	H		N	E	E	D	Y
O	R	G	A	N		S	O	Y	A		A	G	E	
			M	A	H	I		C	O	S	T	N	E	R
S	E	S	S	I	O	N	S		U	T	E	S		
E	M	T		W	N	W		R	A	S	P	E	D	
L	I	R	A		T	O	U	G	H		T	R	U	E
F	R	I	S	C	O		N	R	A		A	R	A	
	P	I	A	F		G	U	I	L	T	Y	O	F	
O	C	T	A	V	I	A		B	R	I	O			
P	O	E		E	X	P	O		L	U	C	I	A	
A	M	A	N	A		H	O	N	E	Y	C	O	M	B
R	E	S	E	T		I	Z	O	D		A	L	A	I
T	R	E	E	S		D	E	M	S		N	E	X	T

46

```
R I C ■ ■ N A D I A ■ S I L L
E N O W ■ I S I N G ■ A S E A
C A S A B L A N C A ■ X R A Y
I N T R A ■ ■ A T T ■ A D S ■
T E A M M A T E ■ H O P E R ■
E R S T ■ N A S ■ A N A L O G
■ ■ ■ O C T E T S ■ S M I L E
C A R ■ H I B A C H I ■ S E E
I R E N E ■ O T O O L E ■ ■ ■
A T D A W N ■ E R R ■ M A I L
■ O S H E A ■ S E A H O R S E
K F C ■ D I X ■ ■ A T E I N ■
A W A Y ■ A T B O T H E N D S
R A R E ■ D R O N E ■ D A R E
T R E S ■ S A X O N ■ ■ S O S
```

47

```
S O L O N G ■ G O T T A R U N
T R I B A L ■ O K A Y B Y M E
R A M O N A ■ P I C K I E S T
A T P E A C E ■ E K E D ■ ■ ■
T O E ■ ■ E E R ■ ■ ■ E B B S
A R R A Y ■ L O B B Y ■ E Y E
■ ■ ■ L O A ■ S A Y O N A R A
F A M O U S L A S T W O R D S
A U R E V O I R ■ E L L ■ ■ ■
I R E ■ E N D I T ■ S O B E R
L A D S ■ ■ O A K ■ ■ A V E ■
■ ■ ■ A D D S ■ S A T I R E S
H A S B E E N S ■ B I S T R O
I S U R E C A N ■ O N E A L L
T I M E T O G O ■ B Y E B Y E
```

48

```
S A L U D ■ C R A N E ■ D E B
A B A S E ■ O I L E R ■ U N O
L O B S T E R P O T S ■ P E P
T O O T ■ V A S E S ■ H O S E
■ ■ R E B E L ■ S I N C E ■ ■
N O D E A L ■ B A C K S T O P
O R A L S ■ S A M E A S ■ ■ ■
W R Y ■ S U N S P O T ■ B R O
■ ■ D E F I E S ■ I B E A M ■
T A N K T O P S ■ I N L A W S
O V E N S ■ ■ E G G O N ■ ■ ■
D E W Y ■ P E D R O ■ O P I E
A N A ■ N E W Y O R K P O S T
T U G ■ B R E E D ■ F E L L A
E E E ■ C U R S E ■ C R E E L
```

49

```
E S P E R A N T O ■ W A T C H
C O U T U R I E R ■ A N G L E
H O T C R O S S B U N N I E S
O N T ■ ■ M I S ■ ■ S T U F F S
■ ■ ■ P D A ■ ■ D E A L ■ ■ ■
H I G H E S T B I D D I E S ■
A N O D E ■ A E R O S ■ N A G
H I S S ■ A L I E N ■ A L B A
N N E ■ O P E N S ■ A B A L L
■ K E E P I N G T A B B I E S
■ ■ ■ D U C T ■ ■ F E E ■ ■ ■
A W H I L E ■ A I L ■ ■ M M E
W H I T E S O X F A N N I E S
L A Y O N ■ C L A M B A K E S
S M A R T ■ T E T E A T E T E
```

50

```
T O S C A ■ S C R I P ■ M O N
G R I L L ■ T E A R S ■ C E E
I D G I V E Y O U M Y ■ E D T
■ I N M A N ■ L A C O N I C
O N E A ■ O P S ■ H A R P O
M A R X ■ S E U S S ■ S O U S
E L S E S ■ S N A G S ■ E S T
■ ■ S E A T B U T I M ■ ■ ■
A C T ■ P A L E D ■ N O A H S
N O R M ■ S E L I G ■ B R O S
C H I C O ■ T S O ■ I M U S
H A V A R T I ■ W A L E D ■
O B I ■ S I T T I N G I N I T
R I A ■ O V E N S ■ E Z I N E
S T L ■ N O R T H ■ R E A I M
```

51

W	I	V	E	S	■	F	A	C	T	■	B	I	K	E
E	M	I	L	E	■	I	N	O	R	■	U	K	E	S
S	M	A	L	L	■	D	I	M	E	■	R	E	N	T
L	U	C	I	L	L	E	S	B	A	L	L	■	■	■
E	N	O	S	■	O	L	E	A	T	E	■	T	A	U
Y	O	M	■	S	C	I	■	T	Y	C	O	O	N	S
■	■	■	S	P	A	T	E	■	T	I	L	D	E	■
■	S	A	L	L	Y	S	F	I	E	L	D	■	■	■
S	N	A	F	U	■	P	A	R	R	Y	■	■	■	■
P	O	W	E	R	P	C	■	C	A	N	■	G	A	M
A	D	S	■	G	R	A	V	E	N	■	A	R	N	O
■	■	N	E	I	L	S	D	I	A	M	O	N	D	■
L	E	G	O	■	O	L	I	O	■	L	O	U	I	E
I	R	I	S	■	R	A	G	U	■	M	U	S	E	S
Z	A	N	Y	■	I	S	N	T	■	A	R	E	S	T

52

G	A	B	S	■	C	A	V	S	■	R	A	H	A	L
A	L	L	A	■	A	L	E	C	■	O	R	O	N	O
R	E	A	M	■	V	E	E	R	■	M	I	L	N	E
T	R	I	P	L	E	S	P	A	C	E	■	Y	A	W
H	O	R	R	O	R	■	■	M	I	R	A	C	L	E
■	■	■	A	G	N	E	W	■	R	O	A	R	■	■
P	E	P	S	I	■	L	A	I	C	■	H	O	C	K
A	L	A	■	C	O	O	L	C	A	T	■	S	H	E
W	I	T	H	■	P	I	K	E	■	H	O	S	E	A
■	■	T	A	U	T	■	S	T	A	R	T	■	■	■
O	L	Y	M	P	I	C	■	■	P	O	T	P	I	E
S	O	C	■	S	C	H	O	O	L	B	O	A	R	D
C	O	A	T	I	■	A	R	G	O	■	M	B	A	S
A	S	K	E	D	■	M	A	R	M	■	A	L	T	E
R	E	E	C	E	■	P	L	E	B	■	N	O	E	L

53

E	X	C	E	L	■	S	E	L	M	A	■	B	B	C
L	E	O	X	I	■	A	R	O	A	R	■	A	O	L
F	R	E	E	Z	E	F	R	A	M	E	■	N	A	E
■	■	■	C	A	R	E	■	M	A	N	D	A	T	E
T	O	F	U	■	A	S	H	■	B	A	I	N	E	S
U	N	I	T	A	S	■	A	S	E	■	V	A	L	E
B	A	R	E	S	■	O	T	T	A	W	A	S	■	■
E	N	S	■	T	O	S	P	A	R	E	■	P	J	S
■	T	R	A	N	S	I	T	■	N	O	L	I	E	■
P	O	S	E	■	N	O	N	■	S	T	R	I	V	E
O	C	T	A	V	O	■	S	S	W	■	I	T	E	M
P	A	R	R	O	T	S	■	C	A	T	O	■	■	■
P	S	I	■	T	I	N	P	A	N	A	L	L	E	Y
E	E	K	■	E	C	A	R	D	■	L	E	A	V	E
D	Y	E	■	R	E	P	O	S	■	C	S	P	A	N

54

F	L	A	S	K	■	A	W	E	■	B	E	E	P	S
L	A	C	T	I	■	T	H	E	■	U	L	T	R	A
A	V	E	R	T	■	O	I	L	■	Z	O	N	E	S
B	A	D	A	B	I	N	G	■	E	Z	P	A	S	S
■	■	■	W	A	D	E	■	O	N	C	E	■	■	■
■	F	U	H	G	E	D	A	B	O	U	D	I	T	■
H	A	R	A	S	S	■	B	E	S	T	■	S	A	G
A	N	A	T	■	B	A	Y	■	■	I	L	S	A	■
I	N	N	■	S	P	E	C	■	K	A	R	A	T	S
■	Y	O	U	T	A	L	K	I	N	T	O	M	E	■
■	■	■	P	A	C	T	■	C	O	I	N	■	■	■
B	A	D	D	I	E	■	M	O	B	S	C	E	N	E
O	C	E	A	N	■	B	A	N	■	K	A	R	E	N
E	L	A	T	E	■	U	Z	I	■	E	G	G	E	D
R	U	L	E	D	■	S	E	C	■	T	E	S	T	S

55

S	O	L	A	R	A	■	F	A	T	S	■	A	S	S
T	H	E	F	O	G	■	I	B	E	T	■	D	R	E
E	D	E	R	L	E	■	R	O	N	A	■	O	I	L
P	A	R	O	L	E	R	E	V	E	R	S	A	L	■
P	R	E	P	S	■	I	M	E	T	■	O	N	A	N
E	N	D	O	■	A	S	A	■	S	U	N	N	Y	■
■	■	■	P	A	R	E	N	T	S	T	R	I	K	E
A	L	P	■	B	T	U	■	S	H	A	■	E	A	T
C	I	R	C	U	S	P	A	T	E	N	T	■	■	■
A	F	O	O	T	■	T	R	A	■	A	L	E	R	■
P	E	D	I	■	W	A	W	A	■	S	P	I	N	E
■	B	U	F	F	A	L	O	P	A	W	I	N	G	S
D	O	C	■	I	G	O	R	■	D	O	O	G	I	E
R	A	E	■	E	E	N	S	■	D	O	C	E	N	T
Y	T	D	■	F	R	E	T	■	S	P	A	R	E	S

56

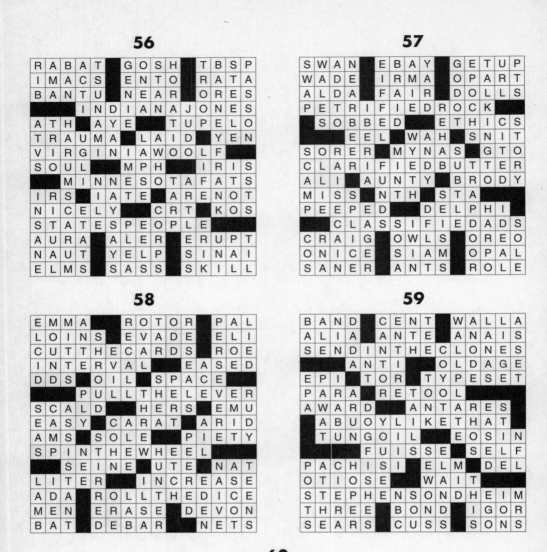

R	A	B	A	T		G	O	S	H		T	B	S	P
I	M	A	C	S		E	N	T	O		R	A	T	A
B	A	N	T	U		N	E	A	R		O	R	E	S
			I	N	D	I	A	N	A	J	O	N	E	S
A	T	H		A	Y	E			T	U	P	E	L	O
T	R	A	U	M	A		L	A	I	D		Y	E	N
V	I	R	G	I	N	I	A	W	O	O	L	F		
S	O	U	L			M	P	H			I	R	I	S
	M	I	N	N	E	S	O	T	A	F	A	T	S	
I	R	S		I	A	T	E		A	R	E	N	O	T
N	I	C	E	L	Y		C	R	T		K	O	S	
S	T	A	T	E	S	P	E	O	P	L	E			
A	U	R	A		A	L	E	R		E	R	U	P	T
N	A	U	T		Y	E	L	P		S	I	N	A	I
E	L	M	S		S	A	S	S		S	K	I	L	L

57

S	W	A	N		E	B	A	Y		G	E	T	U	P
W	A	D	E		I	R	M	A		O	P	A	R	T
A	L	D	A		F	A	I	R		D	O	L	L	S
P	E	T	R	I	F	I	E	D	R	O	C	K		
	S	O	B	B	E	D			E	T	H	I	C	S
			E	E	L		W	A	H		S	N	I	T
S	O	R	E	R		M	Y	N	A	S		G	T	O
C	L	A	R	I	F	I	E	D	B	U	T	T	E	R
A	L	I			A	U	N	T	Y		B	R	O	D	Y
M	I	S	S		N	T	H		S	T	A			
P	E	E	P	E	D			D	E	L	P	H	I	
		C	L	A	S	S	I	F	I	E	D	A	D	S
C	R	A	I	G		O	W	L	S		O	R	E	O
O	N	I	C	E		S	I	A	M		O	P	A	L
S	A	N	E	R		A	N	T	S		R	O	L	E

58

E	M	M	A		R	O	T	O	R		P	A	L
L	O	I	N	S		E	V	A	D	E		E	L	I
C	U	T	T	H	E	C	A	R	D	S		R	O	E
I	N	T	E	R	V	A	L			E	A	S	E	D
D	D	S		O	I	L		S	P	A	C	E		
		P	U	L	L	T	H	E	L	E	V	E	R	
S	C	A	L	D			H	E	R	S		E	M	U
E	A	S	Y		C	A	R	A	T		A	R	I	D
A	M	S		S	O	L	E			P	I	E	T	Y
S	P	I	N	T	H	E	W	H	E	E	L			
		S	E	I	N	E		U	T	E		N	A	T
L	I	T	E	R			I	N	C	R	E	A	S	E
A	D	A		R	O	L	L	T	H	E	D	I	C	E
M	E	N		E	R	A	S	E		D	E	V	O	N
B	A	T		D	E	B	A	R			N	E	T	S

59

B	A	N	D		C	E	N	T		W	A	L	L	A
A	L	I	A		A	N	T	E		A	N	A	I	S
S	E	N	D	I	N	T	H	E	C	L	O	N	E	S
			A	N	T	I			O	L	D	A	G	E
E	P	I		T	O	R		T	Y	P	E	S	E	T
P	A	R	A		R	E	T	O	O	L				
A	W	A	R	D			A	N	T	A	R	E	S	
	A	B	U	O	Y	L	I	K	E	T	H	A	T	
T	U	N	G	O	I	L			E	O	S	I	N
			F	U	I	S	S	E		S	E	L	F
P	A	C	H	I	S	I		E	L	M		D	E	L
O	T	I	O	S	E		W	A	I	T				
S	T	E	P	H	E	N	S	O	N	D	H	E	I	M
T	H	R	E	E		B	O	N	D		I	G	O	R
S	E	A	R	S		C	U	S	S		S	O	N	S

60

S	A	D	A		A	N	I	L		L	O	W	L	Y
T	R	I	S		Z	E	N	O		E	L	I	T	E
I	A	N	S		T	O	N	Y	A	W	A	R	D	S
G	R	E	A	S	E		O	V	I	N	E			
M	A	R	I	A	C	A	L	L	A	S		H	A	L
A	T	O	L	L		M	I	A		R	A	R	E	
			U	P	O	N		E	S	K	I	M	O	
	W	E	S	T	S	I	D	E	S	T	O	R	Y	
B	A	S	K	E	T		S	R	T	A				
E	L	O	I		S	A	G		L	E	R	O	I	
G	E	T		N	E	W	Y	O	R	K	J	E	T	S
	E	M	O	T	E		U	S	E	N	E	T		
C	A	R	D	S	H	A	R	K	S		C	O	L	L
A	R	I	S	E		T	I	E	S		T	I	L	E
D	I	C	E	D		Y	O	Y	O		S	R	O	S

61

```
F E T E . A F A R . D A C H A
A C R E . N A S A . E T H A N
T H E G O O D S H E P H E R D
S O X . D I E T . Q U O T E S
. . V E N D . C U T S . . . .
P A L E S T . G R A Y . C H E
A C E R S . U R A L . W H O A
T H E B A D N E W S B E A R S
T E C S . R I A L . L E O N E
I S H . M I T T . L A P S E D
. . P A V E . H A Z Y . . . .
O C T A N E . J U T E . I C K
T H E U G L Y A M E R I C A N
T E R S E . A V O N . D O M O
O W N E R . M A R T . A N E W
```

62

```
C A S H . S A T I N Y . T E A
O B O E . A T O N C E . A R T
D E M I . L O O K A L I K E S
. . B R E A M . A P I E C E .
F I R . S M I T E . I O T A .
I D E N T I C A L T W I N S .
T E R I . . N I N A . . . . .
. D O P P E L G A N G E R S .
. . I D E E . . V E T S . . .
. S P I T T I N G I M A G E S
S P U D . S T O R E . U T E .
A R M O R S . V I T A L . . .
D U P L I C A T E S . S A T E
A C E . G A L O R E . I R A S
T E D . S T E R N S . A S P S
```

63

```
P S I . A C I D . T H E L M A
O W N . L A Z E . H A V E A T
R E D . S L O B . U N E A S E
T R E E O F D I A M O N D S .
E V E R . . R B I . P E A . .
R E P A S T . S R S . M I N I
. P E A L E . C A P E R . . .
. N O T A T R U S T R E E T .
N I K O N . M E T O O . . . .
O N L Y . G A S . T W I L L S
D E A . S I N . N O O N . . .
. T H E T R I L L I S G O N E
M E O W E D . E A S T . P G A
R E M O V E . N I L E . E E K
S N A K E D . D R E W . D R Y
```

64

```
A B B E . Z E A L . A J A R
T R A X . A D L A I . D E C O
W A S H I N G T O N . A F R O
A V I A R I E S . K N I F E D
R E S U M E S . A W I R E .
. . S A S . P R E V . R E Q
B E R T . E A G L E . S T U
L O O . L I N C O L N . O R E
U N O . A T T E N . O N E S
E S S . U S E S . Y M A .
. E R R O R . B E A R C A T
V I V I A N . B O A T S H O W
A P E D . M T R U S H M O R E
I S L E . E V E N T . A R T E
L O T S . A D D S . N E A T
```

65

```
H A V E N S . S E C . S K I D
I D I D I T . T R Y . K E N O
M A R T H A D A N D R I D G E
O N T . R U R . A P S E S
M O U N T V E R N O N . .
. I R E . O M I C R O N
A M I G O . L O R N . R I P E
V I R G I N I A M I L I T I A
E L A L . A B R A . E S T E R
R O S E L L E . M A T .
. V A L L E Y F O R G E
A L I B I . I A N . A O L
C O N T I N E N T A L A R M Y
E R L E . B A T . H A B E A S
D E A N . C R Y . S T E R N E
```

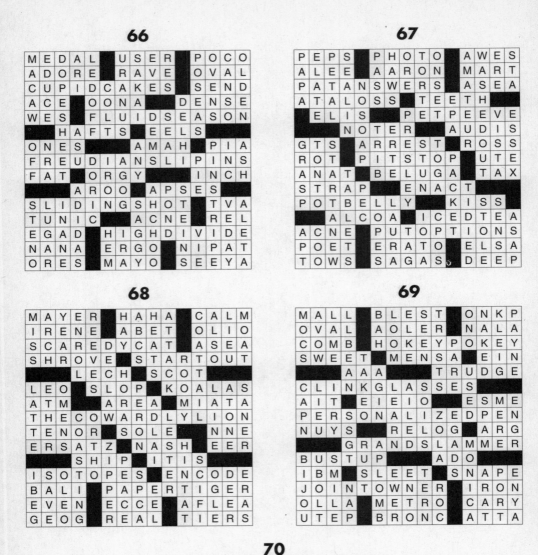

66

MEDAL USER POCO
ADORE RAVE OVAL
CUPIDCAKES SEND
ACE OONA DENSE
WES FLUIDSEASON
HAFTS EELS
ONES AMAH PIA
FREUDIANSLIPINS
FAT ORGY INCH
AROO APSES
SLIDINGSHOT TVA
TUNIC ACNE REL
EGAD HIGHDIVIDE
NANA ERGO NIPAT
ORES MAYO SEEYA

67

PEPS PHOTO AWES
ALEE AARON MART
PATANSWERS ASEA
ATALOSS TEETH
ELIS PETPEEVE
NOTER AUDIS
GTS ARREST ROSS
ROT PITSTOP UTE
ANAT BELUGA TAX
STRAP ENACT
POTBELLY KISS
ALCOA ICEDTEA
ACNE PUTOPTIONS
POET ERATO ELSA
TOWS SAGAS DEEP

68

MAYER HAHA CALM
IRENE ABET OLIO
SCAREDYCAT ASEA
SHROVE STARTOUT
LECH SCOT
LEO SLOP KOALAS
ATM AREA MIATA
THECOWARDLYLION
TENOR SOLE NNE
ERSATZ NASH EER
SHIP ITIS
ISOTOPES ENCODE
BALI PAPERTIGER
EVEN ECCE AFLEA
GEOG REAL TIERS

69

MALL BLEST ONKP
OVAL AOLER NALA
COMB HOKEYPOKEY
SWEET MENSA EIN
AAA TRUDGE
CLINKGLASSES
AIT EIEIO ESME
PERSONALIZEDPEN
NUYS RELOG ARG
GRANDSLAMMER
BUSTUP ADO
IBM SLEET SNAPE
JOINTOWNER IRON
OLLA METRO CARY
UTEP BRONC ATTA

70

GAZE SCAPE SLOW
IGET HABIT PASO
BRIC AMANA OCHO
BATHSHEBA KNEEL
AST FLAGDAY
PATTY OTOOLE
AUGUST ARR CENT
CRIB OCHER AMAH
TAFT ROO ESKIMO
HAMLET HELEN
REFUGEE ESO
AROMA SOAPOPERA
GARP ULTRA ATAD
ETTE SATED GAZA
DOER SWORE ELEM

71

M	A	T	T		S	T	E	A	L		S	A	I	L
A	R	I	A		T	E	S	L	A		E	T	T	U
D	E	E	R		I	N	T	E	L		N	E	A	L
	S	T	I	L	L	E	R	A	N	D	A	L	L	
S	L	O		N	E	B		L	O	A	M	Y		
M	I	N	C	E	S		S	W	A	N	K			
A	T	E	U	P		D	E	A	N			G	A	S
S	H	O	R	T	E	R	A	N	D	S	W	E	E	T
H	E	N			G	I	L	D		P	A	T	S	Y
		L	O	O	P	Y		P	I	S	T	O	N	
	G	I	A	N	T		E	O	N		O	P	E	
H	U	N	T	E	R	A	N	D	P	E	C	K		
A	I	D	E		I	M	A	G	E		U	N	I	T
U	S	E	S		P	E	T	E	Y		T	O	R	O
T	E	X	T		S	N	O	R	E		S	W	A	P

72

A	S	A	I	R		A	C	L	U		T	W	A	S
G	U	I	D	O		R	A	I	N		E	A	T	A
F	I	R	E	S	I	G	N	T	H	E	A	T	R	E
A	T	F		S	K	U	A		E	A	S	E	I	N
		O	K	I	E	S		C	A	M	E	R	A	S
F	A	R	I	N	A		D	O	T	E	L	L		
L	A	C	T	I		C	A	R	E	S		O	W	L
A	R	E	S		O	A	R	E	D		S	O	I	E
P	E	R		A	P	S	I	S		B	O	S	S	A
		E	R	R	A	T	A		D	U	S	T	E	R
A	S	S	A	I	L	S		S	A	M	O	A		
T	H	E	N	C	E		N	E	R	D		T	S	U
E	A	R	T	H	S	H	A	T	T	E	R	I	N	G
I	D	V	E		C	O	P	T		A	B	O	I	L
N	E	E	R		E	S	S	O		L	I	N	T	Y

73

A	L	E	C		A	C	T	U	P		A	D	A	M
T	E	R	I		M	O	U	S	E		V	I	B	E
N	O	T	T	O	B	E	B	E	L	I	E	V	E	D
O	V	E	R	R	I	D	E		L	A	R	V	A	E
		I	C	E		D	E	M		Y	M	A		
H	O	W	C	A	N	T	H	A	T	B	E			
A	P	E		S	C	R	A	P		S	T	E	A	K
L	E	S	S		E	A	R	P	S		C	A	T	O
O	N	T	A	P		D	E	L	T	A		S	R	O
		G	I	V	E	M	E	A	B	R	E	A	K	
S	T	A		Q	E	D		R	N	A				
A	R	M	O	U	R		S	E	L	E	C	T	E	E
Y	O	U	R	E	N	O	T	S	E	R	I	O	U	S
S	O	S	A		A	V	A	S	T		N	O	R	A
O	P	E	L		L	A	G	O	S		E	N	O	S

74

P	A	T	S		M	E	C	C	A		S	H	U	E
A	C	R	E		A	T	A	R	I		K	A	R	L
S	H	E	R	Y	L	C	R	O	W		E	R	I	E
T	E	A	P	O	T			N	A	M	E	T	A	G
A	D	D	E	D		U	N	E		I	T	C	H	Y
			N	A	C	H	O	S		S	E	R		
P	O	E	T		L	O	O		S	T	R	A	F	E
R	I	D		J	O	H	N	J	A	Y		N	O	R
O	L	D	H	A	T		D	U	N		S	E	E	R
		Y	O	N		B	A	N	G	L	E			
C	A	R	T	E		E	Y	E		E	A	S	Y	A
I	N	A	S	T	I	R			F	A	M	O	U	S
G	I	V	E		P	E	T	E	R	F	I	N	C	H
A	S	E	A		S	T	A	L	E		L	A	C	E
R	E	N	T		O	S	S	I	E		E	R	A	S

75

T	E	A	C	U	P		E	T	D		E	R	R	S
E	R	R	O	L	L		S	E	E		N	E	E	T
S	I	R	I	C	A		A	S	S		A	F	A	R
		A	R	E	Y	O	U	S	I	N	C	E	R	E
L	A	Y		R	A	T			A	T	R	E	E	
E	Y	E	C	A	T	C	H	I	N	G		E	N	T
E	N	D	A	T		O	O	O		M	E	D	S	
		S	E	A	C	R	U	I	S	E				
D	U	K	E		J	O	N		U	R	G	E	D	
R	N	A		K	A	Y	E	B	A	L	L	A	R	D
O	S	T	E	O			E	L	L		S	A	S	
W	H	Y	N	O	T	T	H	E	B	E	S	T		
N	A	D	A		R	I	A		E	N	U	R	E	S
E	D	I	T		A	N	T		R	E	F	I	L	L
D	E	D	E		M	T	S		T	R	I	C	K	Y

The New York Times
Crossword Puzzles

The #1 name in crosswords

Available at your local bookstore or online at nytimes.com/nytstore

Coming Soon!

Rise and Shine Crossword Puzzles	0-312-37833-5	$7.95/$8.95 Can.
Coffee, Tea or Crosswords	0-312-37828-9	$7.95/$8.95 Can.
Crosswords for Two	0-312-37830-0	$12.95/$14.95 Can.
Will Shortz Presents I Love Crosswords Vol. 2	0-312-37837-8	$7.95/$8.95 Can.
Crosswords to Keep Your Brain Young	0-312-37658-8	$8.95/$10.50 Can.
Sweet Dreams Crosswords	0-312-37836-X	$9.95/$11.95 Can.
Easy Crossword Puzzles Vol. 9	0-312-37831-9	$9.95/$11.95 Can.
Sunday at Home Crosswords	0-312-37834-3	$7.95/$8.95 Can.
Easy to Not-So-Easy Crossword Puzzle Omnibus Vol. 2	0-312-37832-7	$12.95/$14.95 Can.
Crosswords for a Relaxing Weekend	0-312-37829-7	$12.95/$14.95 Can.

Special Editions

Little Black (and White) Book of Crosswords	0-312-36105-X	$12.95/$14.95 Can.
The Joy of Crosswords	0-312-37510-7	$9.95/$11.95 Can.
Little Red and Green Book of Crosswords	0-312-37661-8	$13.95/$16.25 Can.
Little Flip Book of Crosswords	0-312-37043-1	$10.95/$12.75 Can.
How to Conquer the New York Times. Crossword Puzzle	0-312-36554-3	$9.95/$11.95 Can.
Will Shortz's Favorite Crossword Puzzles	0-312-30613-X	$9.95/$11.95 Can.
Will Shortz's Favorite Sunday Crossword Puzzles	0-312-32488-X	$9.95/$11.95 Can.
Will Shortz's Greatest Hits	0-312-34242-X	$8.95/$10.50 Can.
Will Shortz Presents Crosswords for 365 Days	0-312-36121-1	$9.95/$11.95 Can.
Will Shortz's Funniest Crossword Puzzles	0-312-32489-8	$9.95/$11.95 Can.
Will Shortz's Funniest Crossword Puzzles Vol. 2	0-312-33960-7	$9.95/$11.95 Can.
Will Shortz's Xtreme Xwords	0-312-35203-4	$7.95/$8.95 Can.
Vocabulary Power Crosswords	0-312-35199-2	$10.95/$12.75 Can.

Daily Crosswords

Fitness for the Mind Crosswords Vol. 1	0-312-34955-6	$10.95/$12.75 Can.
Fitness for the Mind Crosswords Vol. 2	0-312-35278-6	$10.95/$12.75 Can.
Crosswords for the Weekend	0-312-34332-9	$9.95/$11.95 Can.
Daily Crossword Puzzles Vol. 71	0-312-34858-4	$9.95/$11.95 Can.
Daily Crossword Puzzles Vol. 72	0-312-35260-3	$9.95/$11.95 Can.

Volumes 57-70 also available

Easy Crosswords

Easy Crossword Puzzles Vol. 8	0-312-36558-6	$9.95/$11.95 Can.
Easy Crossword Puzzles Vol. 7	0-312-35261-1	$9.95/$11.95 Can.
Easy Crossword Puzzles Vol. 6	0-312-33057-7	$9.95/$11.95 Can.

Volumes 2-5 also available

Tough Crosswords

Tough Crossword Puzzles Vol. 13	0-312-34240-3	$10.95/$12.75 Can.
Tough Crossword Puzzles Vol. 12	0-312-32442-1	$10.95/$12.75 Can.
Tough Crossword Puzzles Vol. 11	0-312-31456-6	$10.95/$12.75 Can.

Volumes 9-10 also available

Sunday Crosswords

Simply Sunday Crosswords	0-312-34243-8	$7.95/$8.95 Can.
Sunday in the Park Crosswords	0-312-35197-6	$7.95/$8.95 Can.
Sunday Morning Crossword Puzzles	0-312-35672-2	$7.95/$8.95 Can.
Everyday Sunday Crossword Puzzles	0-312-36106-8	$7.95/$8.95 Can.
Sunday Brunch Crosswords	0-312-36557-8	$7.95/$8.95 Can.
Sunday at the Seashore Crosswords	0-312-37070-9	$7.95/$8.95 Can.
Sleepy Sunday Crossword Puzzles	0-312-37508-5	$7.95/$8.95 Can.
Sunday's Best	0-312-37637-5	$7.95/$8.95 Can.
Sunday Crossword Puzzles Vol. 33	0-312-37507-7	$9.95/$11.95 Can.
Sunday Crossword Puzzles Vol. 32	0-312-36066-5	$9.95/$11.95 Can.
Sunday Crossword Puzzles Vol. 31	0-312-34862-2	$9.95/$11.95 Can.

Large-Print Crosswords

Large-Print Big Book of Holiday Crosswords	0-312-33092-8	$12.95/$14.95 Can.
Large-Print Crosswords for a Brain Workout	0-312-32612-2	$10.95/$12.75 Can.
Large-Print Crosswords for Your Coffee Break	0-312-33109-6	$10.95/$12.75 Can.
Large-Print Will Shortz's Favorite Crossword Puzzles	0-312-33959-3	$10.95/$12.75 Can.
Large-Print Crosswords to Boost Your Brainpower	0-312-32037-X	$10.95/$12.75 Can.
Large-Print Daily Crossword Puzzles	0-312-32037-X	$10.95/$12.75 Can.
Large-Print Daily Crossword Puzzles Vol. 2	0-312-33111-8	$10.95/$12.75 Can.
Large-Print Crosswords for Your Bedside	0-312-34245-4	$10.95/$12.75 Can.
Large-Print Big Book of Easy Crosswords	0-312-33958-5	$12.95/$14.95 Can.
Large-Print Easy Crossword Omnibus Vol. 1	0-312-32439-1	$12.95/$14.95 Can.
Large-Print Crossword Puzzle Omnibus Vol. 8	0-312-37514-X	$13.95/$14.95 Can.
Large-Print Crossword Puzzle Omnibus Vol. 7	0-312-36125-4	$12.95/$14.95 Can.
Large-Print Crossword Puzzle Omnibus Vol. 6	0-312-34861-4	$12.95/#16.25 Can.

Omnibus

Easy to Not-So-Easy Crossword Omnibus Vol. 1	0-312-37516-6	$12.95/$14.95 Can.
Crosswords for a Lazy Afternoon	0-312-33108-8	$12.95/$14.95 Can.
Lazy Weekend Crossword Puzzle Omnibus	0-312-34247-0	$12.95/$14.95 Can.
Lazy Sunday Crossword Puzzle Omnibus	0-312-35279-4	$12.95/$14.95 Can.
Big Book of Holiday Crosswords	0-312-33533-4	$12.95/$14.95 Can.
Giant Book of Holiday Crosswords	0-312-34927-0	$12.95/$14.95 Can.
Ultimate Crossword Omnibus	0-312-31622-4	$12.95/$14.95 Can.
Tough Crossword Puzzle Omnibus Vol. 1	0-312-32441-3	$12.95/$14.95 Can.
Crossword Challenge	0-312-33951-8	$12.95/$14.95 Can.
Crosswords for a Weekend Getaway	0-312-35198-4	$12.95/$14.95 Can.
Biggest Beach Crossword Omnibus	0-312-35667-6	$12.95/$14.95 Can.
Weekend Away Crossword Puzzle Omnibus	0-312-35669-2	$12.95/$14.95 Can.
Weekend at Home Crossword Puzzle Omnibus	0-312-35670-6	$12.95/$14.95 Can.
Holiday Cheer Crossword Puzzles	0-312-36126-2	$12.95/$14.95 Can.
Crosswords for a Long Weekend	0-312-36560-8	$12.95/$14.95 Can.
Crosswords for a Relaxing Vacation	0-312-36694-9	$12.95/$14.95 Can.
Will Shortz Presents Fun in the Sun Crossword Puzzle Omnibus	0-312-37041-5	$12.95/$14.95 Can.
Sunday Crossword Omnibus Vol. 9	0-312-35666-8	$12.95/$14.95 Can.
Sunday Crossword Omnibus Vol. 8	0-312-32440-5	$12.95/$14.95 Can.
Sunday Crossword Omnibus Vol. 7	0-312-30950-3	$12.95/$14.95 Can.
Easy Crossword Puzzle Omnibus Vol. 5	0-312-34859-2	$12.95/$14.95 Can.
Easy Crossword Puzzle Omnibus Vol. 4	0-312-33537-7	$12.95/$14.95 Can.
Easy Crossword Puzzle Omnibus Vol. 3	0-312-36123-8	$12.95/$14.95 Can.
Crossword Puzzle Omnibus Vol. 16	0-312-36104-1	$12.95/$14.95 Can.
Crossword Puzzle Omnibus Vol. 15	0-312-34856-8	$12.95/$14.95 Can.
Crossword Puzzle Omnibus Vol. 14	0-312-33534-2	$12.95/$14.95 Can.
Supersized Book of Easy Crosswords	0-312-35277-8	$14.95/$17.25 Can.
Supersized Book of Sunday Crosswords	0-312-36122-X	$15.95/$18.50 Can.

Previous volumes also available

Variety Puzzles

Acrostic Puzzles Vol. 10	0-312-34853-3	$9.95/$11.95 Can.
Acrostic Puzzles Vol. 9	0-312-30949-X	$9.95/$11.95 Can.
Sunday Variety Puzzles	0-312-30059-X	$9.95/$11.95 Can.

Portable Size Format

Crosswords for Your Coffee Break	0-312-28830-1	$7.95/$8.95 Can.
Sun, Sand and Crosswords	0-312-30076-X	$7.95/$8.95 Can.
Weekend Challenge	0-312-30079-4	$7.95/$8.95 Can.
Crosswords for the Holidays	0-312-30603-2	$7.95/$8.95 Can.
Crosswords for the Work Week	0-312-30952-X	$7.95/$8.95 Can.
Crossword for Your Beach Bag	0-312-31455-8	$7.95/$8.95 Can.
Crosswords to Boost Your Brainpower	0-312-32033-7	$7.95/$8.95 Can.
Cuddle Up with Crosswords	0-312-37636-7	$7.95/$8.95 Can.
C Is for Crosswords	0-312-37509-3	$7.95/$8.95 Can.
Crazy for Crosswords	0-312-37513-1	$7.95/$8.95 Can.
Crosswords for a Mental Edge	0-312-37069-5	$7.95/$8.95 Can.
Favorite Day Crosswords: Tuesday	0-312-37072-5	$7.95/$8.95 Can.
Afternoon Delight Crosswords	0-312-37071-9	$7.95/$8.95 Can.
Crosswords Under the Covers	0-312-37044-X	$7.95/$8.95 Can.
Crosswords for the Beach	0-312-37073-3	$7.95/$8.95 Can.
Will Shortz Presents I Love Crosswords	0-312-37040-7	$7.95/$8.95 Can.
Will Shortz Presents Crosswords to Go	0-312-36695-7	$7.95/$8.95 Can.
Favorite Day Crosswords: Monday	0-312-36556-X	$7.95/$8.95 Can.
Crosswords in the Sun	0-312-36555-1	$7.95/$8.95 Can.
Expand Your Mind Crosswords	0-312-36553-5	$7.95/$8.95 Can.
After Dinner Crosswords	0-312-36559-4	$7.95/$8.95 Can.
Groovy Crossword Puzzles from the '60s	0-312-36103-3	$7.95/$8.95 Can.
Piece of Cake Crosswords	0-312-36124-6	$7.95/$8.95 Can.
Carefree Crosswords	0-312-36102-5	$7.95/$8.95 Can.
Fast and Easy Crossword Puzzles	0-312-35629-3	$7.95/$8.95 Can.
Backyard Crossword Puzzles	0-312-35668-4	$7.95/$8.95 Can.
Easy Crossword Puzzles for Lazy Hazy Crazy Days	0-312-35671-4	$7.95/$8.95 Can.
Brainbuilder Crosswords	0-312-35276-X	$7.95/$8.95 Can.
Stress-Buster Crosswords	0-312-35196-8	$7.95/$8.95 Can.
Super Saturday Crosswords	0-312-30604-0	$7.95/$8.95 Can.
Café Crosswords	0-312-34854-1	$7.95/$8.95 Can.
Crosswords for Your Lunch Hour	0-312-34857-6	$7.95/$8.95 Can.
Easy as Pie Crossword Puzzles	0-312-34331-0	$7.95/$8.95 Can.
Crosswords to Soothe Your Soul	0-312-34244-6	$7.95/$8.95 Can.
More Quick Crosswords	0-312-34246-2	$7.95/$8.95 Can.
Beach Blanket Crosswords	0-312-34250-0	$7.95/$8.95 Can.
Crosswords to Beat the Clock	0-312-33954-2	$7.95/$8.95 Can.
Crosswords for a Rainy Day	0-312-33952-6	$7.95/$8.95 Can.
Crosswords for Stress Relief	0-312-33953-4	$7.95/$8.95 Can.
Cup of Crosswords	0-312-33955-0	$7.95/$8.95 Can.
Crosswords to Exercise Your Brain	0-312-33536-9	$7.95/$8.95 Can.
Crosswords for Your Breakfast Table	0-312-33535-0	$7.95/$8.95 Can.
More Crosswords for Your Bedside	0-312-33612-8	$7.95/$8.95 Can.
T.G.I.F Crosswords	0-312-33116-9	$7.95/$8.95 Can.
Quick Crosswords	0-312-33114-2	$7.95/$8.95 Can.
Planes, Trains and Crosswords	0-312-33113-4	$7.95/$8.95 Can.
More Sun, Sand and Crosswords	0-312-33112-6	$7.95/$8.95 Can.
Crosswords for a Brain Workout	0-312-32610-6	$7.95/$8.95 Can.
A Cup of Tea Crosswords	0-312-32435-9	$7.95/$8.95 Can.
Crosswords for Your Bedside	0-312-32032-9	$7.95/$8.95 Can.
Coffee Break Crosswords	0-312-37515-8	$9.95/$11.95 Can.

Other volumes also available

🦁 St. Martin's Griffin